# STEP TWO - VALUES AND SPIRITUAL DISCIPLINES

## DISCIPLE MANUAL

### HENDRIK J VORSTER

# TABLE OF CONTENT

# WEEK THREE

# WEEK FOUR

# WEEK FIVE

# WEEK SIX

# WEEK SEVEN

# WEEK EIGHT

# WEEK NINE

# DISCIPLESHIP FOUNDATIONS

STEP TWO
VALUES AND SPIRITUAL DISCIPLINES

Disciple Manual

"...His Disciples came to Him, and He began to teach
them."

*Matthew 5:1-2 (NIV)*

Dr. Hendrik J. Vorster

Discipleship Foundations Series

Step 2 – Values and Spiritual Disciplines (Disciple Manual)

By Dr. Hendrik J. Vorster

A practical guide to being a good disciple of Lord Jesus Christ

Apart from this Handbook, you will also need the following items to complete your study:

New International Version, of the Bible.
A pen or pencil to write the answers.
Coloured pencils (red, blue, green and yellow).

*For more copies and information please visit and write to us at:*
www.churchplantinginstitute.com
resources@churchplantinginstitute.com

Any profits from the sale of this course will be used to promote theological education in the third world.

Scripture taken from the HOLY BIBLE (with reference to the Publishers).

ISBN 13-978-1-7338266-3-1

# WEEK ONE

Introduction

# PART I

# INTRODUCTION

When we look at the teachings of Jesus, we see that He started by teaching His disciples the values of the Kingdom. We all live in a certain culture. A culture is determined by the shared embracing of values.

> *"A culture is determined by the shared embracing of predetermined values."*

### Jesus taught His Disciples Values

We all agree that the impact Jesus had on His Disciples, through the way He discipled them, was quite incredible. We would be wise to consider the key essential elements of His teaching of His Disciples. The first two things Jesus taught, and continued to teach His Disciples, was the Values of the Kingdom of God as well as accompanying Spiritual Disciplines, which would keep those values well rooted and maintained in their lives.

.   .   .

When we look at the Gospel of Matthew, we see how Jesus called His Disciples together to teach them:

> Matthew 5:1-2 (NIV) "[5:1] Now when he saw the
> crowds, he went up on a mountainside and sat
> down. His disciples came to him, [2] and he began
> to teach them, saying:"

Jesus sat down with His Disciples and *taught them about the values of the Kingdom of God*, primarily through the Sermon on the Mount, but then throughout His time of discipling them over a three-and-a-half-year period.

The **first phase of Discipleship** deals with us becoming *"Born again,"* and the **second Phase of Discipleship** deals with us *putting down spiritual roots* in our faith through *developing spiritual disciplines* as well as the establishment and *grounding ourselves in the Values of the Kingdom of God.*

## Each kingdom has its own Culture built on commonly shared values.

Jesus came to establish the Kingdom of God. *Each kingdom has its own culture that is built on commonly shared values.* When we become children of God, we transition from the Kingdom of this world to the Kingdom of our Lord and Saviour, Jesus Christ. The Kingdom of God has its own values. The first thing we need to learn, once we laid a solid Foundation for our Faith to grow in Jesus Christ, is the Values of the Kingdom of God, and how to affirm them in our lives.

A few years ago, we migrated from South Africa to Australia. It was quite a process, one that I don't recommend to the faint-hearted, unless following the Call of God to do so. Once our qualifications, health checks and police clearances were accessed and accepted, we were granted residency visas in Australia, However, when we wanted to become Citizens, we were required to learn, adopt and accept the cultural values of the Australian people, before we could become Citizens.

The Kingdom of God operates on the same principle of us having to accept the values and practices before the blessings of the Kingdom could be enjoyed. Jesus started the process of making His Disciples by teaching them the Values of the Kingdom of God, as well as Spiritual Disciplines that would keep those Values intact.

**Cultures change through the _____ that are upheld.**

Todd Wilson, in his Book "*Dream Big*" explores the changing of a culture and states that there are primarily three ingredients to successful culture change: Values, Narratives and Behavior.[1] He defines these as:

> "Values. Our core _____ reflect what we really care about deep down. They are the things so important to us that they shape our thoughts and our actions. Our values overflow to shape the _____ of our mouth (our narrative) and the _____ of our hands (our behaviours)."
>
> "Our narratives are shaped by the language we use, the stories we tell, and how frequently we talk about and celebrate the things most important to us. Our narratives inspire others to embrace our values and engage on common mission with us."
>
> "Our behaviours are the things we _____, including how and where we invest the time, talent, and financial resources entrusted to our care."[2]

Dr. Ralph Neighbour, or "uncle Ralph" as I affectionately known him, emphasised this area as one of the most important areas to develop in the making of a Disciple. He states, in his Book "Life Basic Training," that "*your beliefs mold your values, which directly influences your actions.*"[3]

*"Your _____ mould your values, which directly influences your actions."*
    *Dr. Ralph W. Neighbour Jr.*

**John the Baptist demanded the demonstration of a change of _____ prior to Baptism.**

For John the Baptist it was more important to baptise people who had a heart change, than baptising those who simply wanted to appear, on the outside and in front of the crowds, to have changed.

On one occasion he firmly addressed the crowds coming to be baptised, questioning the reason for their desire to be baptised. I love the way the Amplified Bible expounds on this powerful message. His message was clear: *"Bear fruit consistent with the trees you've become as a result of your conversion."*

> Luke 3:8 (AMP) "[8] Bear fruits that are deserving and consistent with [your] repentance [that is, conduct worthy of a heart changed, a heart abhorring sin]. And do not begin to say to yourselves, we have Abraham as our father; for I tell you that God is able from these stones to raise up descendants for Abraham."

**Jesus demanded a _____ heart to express itself through a changed life.**

For Jesus it was the assimilation of the Kingdom of God Values, which showed the world that true conversion took place. He both affirmed John's message and continually got to the core of Disciple-ship training by speaking of good and bad trees and the *required consistency between the tree and its fruit.*

> Matthew 7:17-18, 20 (NKJV) "17 Even so, every good tree bears good fruit, but a bad tree bears bad fruit. 18 A

good tree cannot bear bad fruit, nor can a bad tree
bear good fruit. 20 Therefore by their fruits you
will know them."

*"The spiritual roots we develop will determine the fruit we bear,
which will be consistent with the trees we are."*

The assimilation of Kingdom values, consistent with the conversion that took place inside of us, will have an outward effect on the "fruit" we bear. As we allow the Love of God to shine into our hearts, His Love will be experienced by others (the world,) and it will show that we are His Disciples.

John 13:35 (NIV) "35 By this everyone will know that
you are my disciples, if you love one another."

**Jesus called us to teach our Disciples what He taught His.**

Finding Disciples is one thing, but *"teaching them to observe"* is another. Jesus called us to teach our Disciples the very things He taught His Disciples.

**Have you ever wondered where to start?**

I always wondered where to start once people committed their lives to Christ, however when I looked at how Jesus did it, remembering that He started His Discipleship journey with people who left everything to follow Him, I found that Jesus started by teaching His Disciples the Values of the Kingdom of God, and simultaneously spiritual Disciplines.

Developing Spiritual Disciplines is like putting down spiritual roots. The result will be that as you learn and apply the Values of the Kingdom of God, you will bear fruit that will let everyone know the Vine you are grafted into.

**Values are built into our lives by being _____.**

Values are those virtues, which have been added into our lives by intention. Embracing and living godly values build our character. Our character defines us. We are characterised by those values we have adopted and allowed to take root in us. God desires for us to be intentional, both on contemplation as well as application.

> James 1:25 (NIV) 25 But whoever looks intently into the perfect law that gives freedom, and continues in it —not forgetting what they have heard, but doing it —they will be blessed in what they do.

*"Our intentional pursuits become life attributes, qualities, traits and characteristics. We are characterised by those values we have adopted and allowed to take root in us."*

**Values are embraced in our _____ first, before they become part of our hearts, and ultimately our actions.**

One famous writer suggests in one of her books that our bodies follow where our minds go. What we think about and give our attention to, is what we will become. Proverbs says: *"As a man think in his heart, so is he."*

> Philippians 4:8 "Finally, brethren, whatsoever things are true, whatsoever things are honest, whatsoever things are just, whatsoever things are pure, whatsoever things are lovely, whatsoever things are of good report; if there be any virtue, and if there be any praise, think on these things."
> Psalm 119:56 (NIV) "56 This has been my practice: I obey your precepts."

**Values become part of our lives by _____.**

The Apostle Paul taught his spiritual son, Timothy, to have a disciplined life and to pursue godliness.

> 1 Timothy 4:7 (NIV) "Have nothing to do with godless
> myths and old wives' tales;
> rather, train yourself to be godly."

> *"Values are the fruit we bear from the decisions we make, through our pursuits of following the example of Christ."*

**We establish Spiritual _____ when we develop Spiritual Disciplines and Kingdom Values.**

> *"Building Values and developing Spiritual Disciplines concurrently, establishes _____ from which our faith will grow and mature."*

Having strong roots are essential to growing a healthy and stable spiritual life. Let us now take a journey into an understanding of Spiritual Disciplines and the Values of the Kingdom of God.

In each weekly lesson there will be a Spiritual Discipline to learn as well as some Kingdom Values. Let us take a few moments and look at each of these two main parts individually.

## Part One - Spiritual Disciplines

> *"Spiritual disciplines are habits, practices, and experiences that are designed to develop, grow, and strengthen our inner man." Dr. Hendrik J. Vorster*

*Spiritual Disciplines will ensure that we retain and maintain the Values we assimilate in our lives.* Spiritual disciplines are habits, practices, and experiences that are designed to develop, grow, and strengthen our inner man. Spiritual disciplines build the capacity of our character and keep the values we aspire to assimilate into our lives, intact. Spiritual disciplines form the structure within which we train our soul to obey. Developing Spiritual Disciplines is like putting down roots into the places where you desire to draw your sustenance from. The Disciplines we develop will become pathways through which God will bring daily and consistent nourishment for our up building and strengthening.

**Values are birthed and developed in our lives by being rooted in a disciplined lifestyle of _____ disciplines.**

Jesus emphasised the value of the development of spiritual roots through the Parable of the Sower. What Jesus taught His Disciples was that, as soon as what the seed of the Word was sown and germinated, Believers need to put down roots to sustain themselves to endure the trouble and persecution that would come on them as a consequence of their decision to follow Christ.

> Psalms 1:3 (NIV) "[3] They are like trees along a
> riverbank bearing luscious fruit each season
> without fail. Their leaves shall never wither, and all
> they do shall prosper.

> Jeremiah 17:7-8 (NIV) "[7] But blessed is the man who
> trusts in the Lord and has made the Lord his hope
> and confidence. [8] He is like a tree planted along a
> riverbank, with its roots reaching deep into the
> water—a tree not bothered by the heat nor worried
> by long months of drought. Its leaves stay green,
> and it goes right on producing all its luscious fruit."

**Put down roots in the right _____**

Everything that grows has roots. The bigger the tree, the deeper and stronger the roots grow. We all grow and put down roots to sustain the life we want to live. Putting down roots through life habits and practices, in the right places, is essential to living a fulfilled and fruitful life.

**Putting down roots take _____.**

We make time for the things we value. When we value spending time with God and love reading and meditating on His Word, we put our hope and confidence in Him to guide and direct us. By spending time with God, because we highly value His guidance and direction, we literally place our hope in Him. There are huge rewards for putting your hope and confidence in Him; it is that putting down of spiritual roots deep into the spiritual resources of God.

> Matthew 13:5-6 (NIV) "Some fell on rocky places, where it did not have much soil. It sprang up quickly, because the soil was shallow. But when the sun came up, the plants were scorched, and they withered because they had no root."

> Matthew 13:20-21 (NIV) "The seed falling on rocky ground refers to someone who hears the word and at once receives it with joy. But since they have no root, they last only a short time. When trouble or persecution comes because of the word, they quickly fall away."

**Develop _____ roots**

Spiritual Disciplines are really the roots from which we will grow. When we are rooted in the right place, we will grow. Having, and developing, spiritual roots in the right practices and disciplines will most certainly ensure a lifetime of healthy growth and an unending fruit bearing life. It is essential to disciple new Believers into an understanding of – and the development of - the spiritual disciplines.

> Romans 11:16 (NIV) "if the part of the dough offered as
> firstfruits is holy, then the whole batch is holy; if
> the root is _____, so are the branches."

If you invest time in evil things, don't be surprised when evil habits, characteristics and behaviour pops up in your life. By spending time and watching bad moral movies, television programs; or spending time with the wrong friends; or reading the wrong books, blogs or websites, is investing into roots that will not bring forth good fruit or develop the good, godly nature you desire.

If you invest time intentionally into developing a good and godly character, built on good moral values, and being a good role model for others to follow, then you will invest time into eternally lasting practices.

**Roots are determined by what you _____ and give _____ to**

We all aspire to be people of high integrity, with well-balanced personalities, good character, and pleasant to be around with natures. You develop the character, nature and behaviour you aspire for by investing time and disciplined practice into developing that character.

What we learn here is both the importance of having "holy roots," but also the impact holy roots have on the branches and ultimately on the fruit it will bear. The Apostle Paul addresses this same matter with the church in Colossae. He exhorts them to *"continue to live their lives in Him"*. How? *"By being rooted and built up in Him."*

> Colossians 2:6-7 (NIV) "So then, just as you received
> Christ Jesus as Lord, continue to live your lives in
> Him, rooted and built up in Him, strengthened in
> the faith as you were taught, and overflowing with
> thankfulness."

This same message is brought to the church in Ephesus; the message of "**being rooted**".

> Ephesians 3:17 (NIV) "so that Christ may dwell in your
> hearts through faith. And I pray that you, being
> rooted and established in love,"

**When we develop spiritual disciplines, we develop spiritual**
**_____.**

The Apostle Paul taught his disciple, Timothy, to train himself to be godly. Developing spiritual disciplines is to train oneself to be godly. What we learn from the Bible is that it is essential equip yourself, train yourself, and develop yourself in Him. The duty is ours to develop a disciplined walk with God.

> 1 Timothy 4:7 (NIV) "7 Have nothing to do with godless
> myths and old wives' tales; rather, train yourself to
> be godly."

### New Testament Practitioners

It seems from the impact that the early Church had that they had a few practices, which positioned them for an atmosphere where people were added to the Church on a daily basis. We also have a number of examples from that of the spiritual Disciplines of the Apostles. As the Church grew the complexities of ministry grew, however, what set the Apostles apart was their discipline to keep their Spiritual Disciplines undisturbed.

Almost on every occasion the Apostles are mentioned it is connected with them going for prayer, busy praying or as a result of them praying and ministering the Word of God that awesome things happened.

∽

Acts 6:4 (NIV) "4 and we will give our attention to
prayer and the ministry of the word."

Acts 2 verses 42-46 highlight some of the spiritual practices of the
Believers in the Book of Acts.

> Acts 2:42-47 (NIV) "42 They devoted themselves to the
> apostles' teaching and to fellowship, to the
> breaking of bread and to prayer. 43 Everyone was
> filled with awe at the many wonders and signs
> performed by the apostles. 44 All the believers
> were together and had everything in common. 45
> They sold property and possessions to give to
> anyone who had need. 46 Every day they
> continued to meet together in the temple courts.
> They broke bread in their homes and ate together
> with glad and sincere hearts, 47 praising God and
> enjoying the favor of all the people. And the Lord
> added to their number daily those who were being
> saved."

In this portion of Scripture we observe at least seven spiritual
disciplines, which existed in the early Church. They practiced these
disciplines daily. They gave themselves to it wholly. The Spiritual
Disciplines of devoting yourself to the Word of God (*Apostle's Teach-ings*), worship (*fellowship*), Communion (*Breaking of Bread*), Prayer,
Simplicity (*had everything in common*), Stewardship (*They sold prop-erty and possessions to give to anyone who had need*) and Witnessing
(*enjoying the favor of all the people.*) The amazing thing about this
testimony and example is that the Lord crowned their private and
corporate devotion, by "*daily adding to their numbers those who were
being saved.*"

Through the coming weeks, we will, each week, explore and
develop one Spiritual Discipline, as well as explore some Values of
the Kingdom of God to assimilate into our lives. I pray that you too

will be *"rooted in Christ,"* and that you will grow into a mighty *"Oak of righteousness."*

## Part Two - Values

*"_____ are the fruit we bear; of the Faith we profess and practice."*

Every Family has family values. Our lives are built upon these values. Values are the fruit we bear, affirming our allegiance and reliance on God. It is that constant demonstration of our faith and the foundation we built our lives on.

I pray that you will be intentional in building these Values into your life, as it will become one of the biggest testimonies you will carry, in your life, of the Power of God to change lives. *Very few things have such incredible convincing power than a changed life.* Let us not just tell people of Christ; let us live the change He brought into our lives. This is only possible as we connect our Faith in God to the renewal work of the Holy Spirit, through being "Born Again," and learning and applying these Kingdom Values. Enjoy this exhilarating journey!

There are many Values in the Kingdom of God, however, for the purpose of this manual, I narrowed them down to 52 Kingdom Values. You could purchase my Books: *"Values of the Kingdom of God", and "Spiritual Disciplines of the Kingdom of God"* through our website, or straight from Amazon.

## Process of Discipleship:

This journey is made up of a few phases. It is called a Discipleship journey from which you will benefit most if you follow them through systematically from Discipleship One to Discipleship Five. This course will take you at least One Year to complete, however, as with living trees, it takes a lifetime to grow into a mighty tree. By daily drawing sap through our spiritual roots, being firmly grounded in the Word, prayer and in Fellowship, we will grow slowly and steadily.

When we look a little closer at each one of these five phases, we liken it to the Parable of the Sower where we see the first four phases of growth and development outlined, but with an emphasis on the condition of our hearts in receiving the Word of God. My prayer is that you will grow and develop into a hundred-fold, fruit-producing Follower of Jesus.

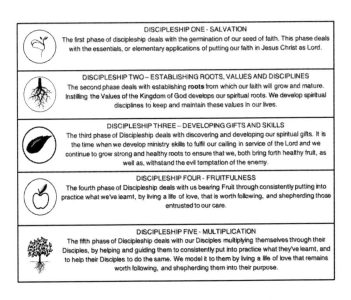

*Process of Discipleship Diagram*

## Process of Discipleship Diagram

This Discipleship Journey is designed for people who desire to, not just receive the Word with gladness, but to receive it and allow it to grow until a multiplied harvest is reaped.

I pray, that through the duration of this discipleship course, you will commit your life to Christ, or, as you go through the sessions, affirm your decision to accept Jesus as the Lord and Saviour of your soul. My prayer for you is that the Word of God, sown through this course, will not be snatched by Satan, but will germinate, take root and grow into maturity, to fruitfulness, and finally to a multiplied life.

> Matthew 13:8 (NIV) "[8] Still other seed fell on good soil, where it produced a crop—a hundred, sixty or thirty times what was sown."

I pray that you will be that person in whose heart the seed of the Word of God will take root, endure through tribulations and persecutions, and persevere through the deceitful, worldly temptations, until you finally become fruitful with souls and see them multiply greatly.

# PART II

# ASSIMILATION SHEET

### Introduction

1. Which are the two essential areas Jesus focused on in His teaching of the Apostles?

_____

_____

2. Complete the sentence. *"Cultures change through the corporate _____ that are upheld."*

3. Complete the sentence. *"Your _____ mould your values, which directly influences your actions."*

4. Complete the sentence. *"John the Baptist demanded the demonstration of the Values prior to_____."*
   Which Scripture tells us about John's demands?_____

. . .

5. By what value will everyone know that we are His Disciples? Give supporting Scripture?

__ _____

_____

6. Complete the sentence. *"Values are built into our lives by being_____."*

7. Complete the sentence. *"Values become part of our lives by_____"*

Give me one Scripture to confirm this? _____

8. Name at least three Spiritual Disciplines that you've learnt about in Acts 2:42-43? _____

_____

_____

_____

# WEEK TWO

# PART I

# SPIRITUAL DISCIPLINES: PRAYER

# 1

## PRAYER

Jesus offered us, and His Disciples advice on *the spiritual discipline of prayer*. He often taught them on this spiritual discipline and He Himself modelled it to them. One of those occasions where He taught them on prayer was in His message on the mountain. Along with teaching His Disciples the values of the Kingdom of God, He also taught them these disciplines.

> Matthew 6:6-8 (NIV) "6 But when you pray, go into
> your room, close the door and pray to your Father,
> who is unseen. Then your Father, who sees what is
> done in secret, will reward you. 7 And when you
> pray, do not keep on babbling like pagans, for they
> think they will be heard because of their many
> words. 8 Do not be like them, for your Father
> knows what you need before you ask him."

> Matthew 6:9-13 (NIV) **9 In this manner**, therefore, **pray:**
> Our Father in heaven, Hallowed be Your name
> **10** Your kingdom come. Your will be done on
> earth as *it is* in heaven.**11** Give us this day our daily

bread. [12] And forgive us our debts, as we forgive
our debtor [13] And do not lead us into temptation,
but deliver us from the evil one. For Yours is the
kingdom and the power and the glory forever.
Amen."

Prayer is the way of communicating with God. Prayer is the dedicated discipline and practice of two-way communication with God. There are many ways to pray and I wish to take a few moments to explore some of these wonderful examples we learn from the Bible.

**How to pray effectively?**

### "Our Father" Prayer

The *"Our Father"* prayer, as taught by the Lord Jesus is one of the most powerful prayers you can ever pray. Here is a summarised explanation to pray it daily.

- *"Our _____ in heaven,"* – As Children of God, we have a Heavenly Father. Address Father God with love and respect as your Father.
- *"Hallowed be Your _____"* - Take time at the beginning of this prayer to honour Father God for who He is to you and what He has done in your live. Praise Him. Worship Him.
- *"May Your _____ come; May Your _____ be done on earth as it is in heaven."* – We confirm that we are part of His Kingdom, and that we desire to see His Kingdom and Rule come into, not only in our lives, but also in the lives of others. We submit ourselves, through this prayer, to do His Will.
- *"Give us today our daily bread."* – We acknowledge our dependency on Him, and recognize Him as the source of

our sustenance. God is our source! He is our Provider, not our own abilities or skills. We declare that He is our source.

- *"And _____ us our sins, as _____ forgive those who sinned against us."* – We all need to forgiveness daily. Take time to confess your sins to Him, and accept the forgiveness that is only found in Christ Jesus. Also take time in prayer to forgive those who sinned against you. The extent to which we forgive is the extent to which we will be forgiven.
- *"And lead us not into temptation, but deliver us from the _____ one."* – We humbly pray that God will protect us from doing or exploring wrong things. We pray for His deliverance from evil things in our lives. We pray for His Divine deliverance, guidance and protection.
- *"For Yours is the _____, and the Power, and the Authority."* – Take time at the end of this short time of prayer to declare again your submission to His Rulership in your life. Take time to declare that He has all the Power and Authority over your life and that of the entire world.

### Tabernacle Prayer

Jesus Christ is our High Priest, serving at the right hand of God, our Father, in Heaven. The Bible teaches that when God gave Moses instruction to build Him a Tabernacle in the Wilderness so that He could dwell among His people, that He needed to build it according to the Pattern God gave him, but also that it was a pattern of the Tabernacle in Heaven.

> Hebrews 8:1-2 (NIV) "1 Now the main point of what we are saying is this: We do have such a high _____, who sat down at the right hand of the throne of the Majesty in heaven, 2 and who serves in the

sanctuary, the true _____ set up by the
Lord, not by a mere human being."

Hebrews 8:5 (NIV) "5 They serve at a sanctuary that is
_____ and shadow of what is in
_____. This is why Moses was warned
when he was about to build the tabernacle: "See to
it that you make everything according to the
pattern shown you on the mountain."

Hebrews 10:19-22 (NIV) "19 Therefore, brothers and
sisters, since we have confidence to enter the Most
Holy Place by the blood of Jesus, 20 by a new and
living way opened for us through the curtain, that
is, his body, 21 and since we have a great priest over
the house of God, 22 let us draw near to God with a
sincere heart and with the full assurance that faith
brings, having our hearts sprinkled to cleanse us
from a guilty conscience and having our bodies
washed with pure water."

The Tabernacle Prayer provides us with a guided pathway of
entering into the Presence of God in a respectable and God-
honouring way. Through these Scriptures we learn that it is actually
one of the ways God desires us to come to Him daily.

- **Gates** – Psalms 100:4 (NIV) says: "*4 Enter his gates with
thanksgiving*" – *Enter your time of prayer, and into the time of
prayer, with thanksgiving in your heart.* Thank God for
whom He is what He means, and have done for you.
Thank Him for the blessings you observe in your life.
Thank Him for being alive, good health, your family, your
church, and the many blessings He has brought into your
life since you last prayed.
- _____ – Psalms 100:4 (NIV) also states: "and his courts

with praise; give thanks to him and praise his name." – Take time to praise Him for whom He is to you. ***This is a great time to declare His Attributes;*** He is My Provider, He is my Protector, He is my Shepherd, He is my Counselor, He is my Righteousness, He is my Guide, He is my Healer and Deliverer, He is the One who is the Mighty God, and whatever you can attribute to Him. It is a time to tell Him what He means to you.

- **Brazen** _____ – The Brazen Altar (Exodus 27:1-8, 38:1-7) is the place in the outer court where burnt offerings was made. The Brazen Altar represents the place where we remember the huge sacrifice Christ paid for our redemption. ***The Brazen Altar is a place in our prayer where we make confession for our sins, and ask for the blood of Jesus to wash us and to clean us*** that we may enter the inner courts with confidence and full assurance that our prayers will be heard and answered. This is a time of applying the Blood of Jesus with reverence and deep gratitude.

- _____ – The Laver (Exodus 30:17) is the place where the Priests were to wash their hands and feet before entering into the Tabernacle. Whereas the Blood of Jesus cleanses us from all unrighteousness, and washes all our sins away, ***the water represents a place where we commit ourselves to live with a clear conscience, and to be committed to live in right standing with God.*** The Laver represents that time during prayer where *we consciously reflect on our ways.* Take time to commit your heart and mind to the Will and Purpose of God. This is also a time to prayerfully consider and ensure that we do not enter into God's Presence with known and hidden sins. One of the key essentials at the Laver is meditating on the 10 Commandments. Ask the Lord for insight into His commandments, review the Scriptures that discuss the commandments both by Moses and as Jesus taught about them in the New Testament.

- **Holy Place** – The first part of the Holy of Holies has three chief furbishments in it: 1. *The Golden Candlestick, 2. The Golden Altar of Incense and 3. The Table of Showbread.* All three play a significant role in the Presence of God and for encountering the Presence of God.

- **The Golden Candlestick** is representative of the _____ **Spirit of God.** (Isaiah 11:2) *We pray for the Power of the Holy Spirit upon our lives.*

We pray for His Wisdom, Insight, and Understanding. We pray for His Counsel, Power and Knowledge in us. We pray for His Gracious Gifts (1Corinthians 12;1-9, and Romans 12) upon us, and present ourselves as His instruments to be used by Him to build the Body of Christ up.

- **The Golden Altar of Incense** is *representative of us bringing prayer and worship, offered in humility and adoration. Our prayers are like sweet smelling fragrances* before the Throne of God. Take time to offer all kinds of intercessions, petitions and other prayers before God.
- **The Table of Showbread** *represents the place that the Word of God, both the Written and Spoken Word of God has in our lives. We take time to meditate on the Word of God, both by what we read as well as what we believe that He has spoken into our lives.* This is especially a place where we listen to hear what God is saying to us. We will not live by bread alone, but by every word from the mouth of God. It is always good to pray with your Bible. Take time to "eat" the Word of God by reading and meditating on it during your time of prayer.

Since Christ died on the Cross, through His Blood the doorway into the Most Holy Place have been opened for us to enter before the Glorious Presence and throne of God. In the Most Holy Place there between the Mercy-seat is the Shekinah Glory of God. Father God is present here in the Most Holy Place. There is only one Furnishment in the most Holy Place and that is the Ark of the Covenant with the Mercy-seat with the Cherubims overshadowing it.

- **Ark of the Covenant** – The Ark of the Covenant represents the Shekinah Glorious Presence of God. In the Ark of the Covenant is three elements:

1. *The ___ Commandments, a constant reminder of the eternal standard of God's Will, but also as a reminder that life in the Presence of God can only be based on the Word and Will of God, and*
2. *The Manna, as representative of God's eternal provision, and sustenance, and*
3. *Aaron's Budding _____, as representative of God's choosing of men from among men, for divine purposes.*

The presence of God surpasses everything and anything that we could ever desire. This is where the most precious Presence of Father God dwells. If it wasn't for the precious Blood of Jesus, who of us could be with Him on His Holy Hill? The Most Holy Place is a place of the Ultimate encounter with Almighty God. It is here that Jesus sits at the right hand of the Father. It is here that Father dwells in all His Shekinah Glory. Take time and let the Lord whisper to you about what He is about to do, as He did with the Apostle John in the Book of Revelation.

Take time in His Presence and let Him give you your daily assignments. It is here in His presence that we worship the Father for His provision of daily manna, His Divine choosing of us, and where we commit ourselves to fulfill His purpose under His authority, and we worship and commit ourselves to His unchangeable standards.

## Praying the Psalms

Another way of Praying is to take your lead from the prayers offered in the Psalms. I regularly read five Psalms a day, and by doing that read and pray through the Psalms in one month. I always find tremendous encouragement as I pray the Psalms as if they were my own words expressed to God.

### Praying the Prayers in the Bible

There are many Prayers in the Bible, as you come across them you can also pray them as if they are your own.

- Jacob prayed when he faced his brother Esau in Genesis 32 verses 9-12.
- Moses prayed
- Abraham prayed
- We have the amazing prayer of Jabez in 1 Chronicles 4 verse 10.
- David prayed many times and places. One of his many prayers is recorded in 2 Samuel 7 verses 18 to 29; it also correlates with 1 Chronicles 17 verses 16 to 27. Most the Psalms that David wrote are his prayers.
- Solomon prayed many prayers such as recorded in 1 Kings 8 verses 22 to 53. We also have the 2 Chronicles 6 verses 12 to 40 prayer. 2 Chronicles 7 is another.
- Daniel prayed in Daniel 9 verses 3 to19. We know that God answered his prayers since we read about it in verses 20 to 23.
- Jesus prayed in John 17.
- Paul's prayer is recorded in Ephesians 1 verses 15 to 21. Ephesians chapter 3, verses 14 to 21, is another prayer. He requested that they pray for him in Ephesians 6 verses 19 to 20.
- John prayed in 3 John 1 verse 2.

### _____ of God Prayer

When we look at Ephesians 6, we read about *the Armour of God*.

This is a great portion of scripture to pray every day. Ephesians 6 verses 13-17 give us an account of this prayer and declaration guideline.

> Ephesians 6: 13-17 (NIV) "[13] Therefore put on the full Armour of God, so that when the day of evil comes, you may be able to stand your ground, and after you have done everything, to stand. [14] Stand firm then, with the belt of truth buckled around your waist, with the breastplate of righteousness in place, [15] and with your feet fitted with the readiness that comes from the gospel of peace. [16] In addition to all this, take up the shield of faith, with which you can extinguish all the flaming arrows of the evil one. [17] Take the helmet of salvation and the sword of the Spirit, which is the word of God.

- *The _____ of Truth* – Embrace and commit to the Truth of God's Word.
- *The Breastplate of Righteousness* – Commit to remain in right standing with God.
- *The _____ of preparedness* – Commit to go where God calls you to go and be His Messenger.
- *The Shield of _____* – Declare your Faith in God above everything else.
- *The _____ of Salvation* – Confirm your Salvation, and commit to offer the message of salvation to others.
- *The Sword of the _____* – Commit to using the Word of God as your weapon against the assaults of the enemy.

### 10 Commandments Prayer

Another great way to pray is to pray the 10 Commandments into your life. Read and Pray Exodus 20:1-17.

Exodus 20:1-17 (NIV) "20 And God spoke all these words: 2 "I am the Lord your God, who brought you out of Egypt, out of the land of slavery. 3 "You shall have no other gods before me. 4 "You shall not make for yourself an image in the form of anything in heaven above or on the earth beneath or in the waters below. 5 You shall not bow down to them or worship them; for I, the Lord your God, am a jealous God, punishing the children for the sin of the parents to the third and fourth generation of those who hate me, 6 but showing love to a thousand generations of those who love me and keep my commandments. 7 "You shall not misuse the name of the Lord your God, for the Lord will not hold anyone guiltless who misuses his name. 8 "Remember the Sabbath day by keeping it holy. 9 Six days you shall labor and do all your work, 10 but the seventh day is a sabbath to the Lord your God. On it you shall not do any work, neither you, nor your son or daughter, nor your male or female servant, nor your animals, nor any foreigner residing in your towns. 11 For in six days the Lord made the heavens and the earth, the sea, and all that is in them, but he rested on the seventh day. Therefore the Lord blessed the Sabbath day and made it holy. 12 "Honor your father and your mother, so that you may live long in the land the Lord your God is giving you. 13 "You shall not murder. 14 "You shall not commit adultery. 15 "You shall not steal. 16 "You shall not give false testimony against your neighbor. 17 "You shall not covet your neighbor's house. You shall not covet your neighbor's wife, or his male or female servant, his ox or donkey, or anything that belongs to your neighbor."

**10 Commandments:**

1. I am the Lord your God; you shall have no other gods before Me.
2. You shall not make idols and worship them.
3. You shall not take the name of the LORD your God in vain.
4. Remember the Sabbath day, to keep it holy.
5. Honor your father and your mother.
6. You shall not murder.
7. You shall not commit adultery.
8. You shall not steal.
9. You shall not bear false witness against your neighbour.
10. You shall not covet your neighbour's wife or any of his possessions.

Commit yourself to keeping the inscribed commands of the Lord in your life through prayer. A Daily Prayer commitment will most certainly keep these basic Commands intact in our lives with the help of the Holy Spirit.

### Praying in the Holy Spirit

When we received the baptism with the Holy Spirit, we also received a prayer language, and that is speaking in tongues.

> 1 Corinthians 14:14-15 (NIV) "14 For if I pray in a tongue, my spirit prays, but my mind is unfruitful. 15 So what shall I do? I will pray with my spirit, but I will also pray with my understanding; I will sing with my spirit, but I will also sing with my understanding."

Jude 1:20-21 (NIV) "20 But you, dear friends, by
building yourselves up in your most holy faith and
praying in the Holy Spirit, 21 keep yourselves in
God's love as you wait for the mercy of our Lord
Jesus Christ to bring you to eternal life."

1 Thessalonians 5:17 KJV "17 Pray without ceasing."

I pray that you will develop this spiritual discipline, and that instead of it being a chore, that it will be that time you set aside each day to be alone with God, and where you will find Mercy and Grace. I pray that your prayers will be answered and that you will be deeply strengthened through spending time with God in prayer.

### Conclusion on Prayer

There are many ways to pray. The posture in prayer is not as important as the heart and devotion with which we pray. Pray daily. Pray with all your heart. Pray!

# PART II

---

# VALUES OF THE KINGDOM
# OF GOD

## 2

# HUMILITY

**Definition:**

_____ is the quality of having a modest or subjected view of one's importance.

**Scriptural teaching:**

> Matthew 5:3 (NIV) 3 "Blessed are the poor in spirit, for theirs is the kingdom of heaven.

> Matthew 5:3 (AMP) [3] "Blessed [spiritually prosperous, happy, to be admired] are the poor in spirit [those devoid of spiritual arrogance, those who regard themselves as insignificant], for theirs is the kingdom of heaven [both now and forever]."

> **1 Peter 5:5-6, Philippians 2:3, Philippians 2:8.**

**Characteristic explained:**

Humility is the first Value or Characteristic Jesus taught His Disciples. A Kingdom operates significantly different from a democratically run country. In a Kingdom there is only One Ruler and doing His or Her will is all that matters. In the Kingdom of God there is One King and His Name is Jesus. In this Kingdom, of which we are part of since being Born Again, doing His Will is the only thing that counts and is prized.

It requires tremendous humility to be a part of a Kingdom. It requires us to whole-heartedly submit and obey everything He said, and through the Holy Spirit's guidance directs us to do. Through submission and whole-hearted obedience, we give expression to our heartfelt humility. This value characterizes every follower of Jesus. We become known for our total submission to His will as taught to us through the Bible.

**Life application:**

The best expression we could give to this value in our lives is to demonstrate it through our subjective and deferent living to the Lordship of Jesus, the Word and the Will of God, in every area of our lives.

# 3

# MOURNFULNESS

**Definition:**

*Mournfulness is the value of penitent, reflective living.* Penitence is the applied value of humbly and honestly assessing one's actions before God, always with a willingness to acknowledge our wrongs and to follow through with repentance. This penitent action reflects the value of mournfulness.

**Scripture:**

> Matthew 5:4 (NIV 1984) 4 Blessed are those who mourn, for they will be comforted.

> Matthew 5:4 (AMP) "4 "Blessed [forgiven, refreshed by God's grace] are those who mourn [over their sins and repent], for they will be comforted [when the burden of sin is lifted].

> Luke 18:13, Psalms 51:1-4.

**Characteristic explained:**

Mournfulness is sometimes described by words like: repentance, remorsefulness, self-reproach, self-accusation, shame, or sorrowfulness. The Matthew Henry Dictionary comments and defines this *"mourning"* as: *"That godly sorrow which works true repentance, watchfulness, a humble mind, and continual dependence for acceptance on the mercy of God in Christ Jesus, with constant seeking the Holy Spirit, to cleanse away the remaining evil, seems here to be intended."* Mournfulness is penitence in action.

**Life Application:**

This value is firmly established in our lives when we always keep ourselves open to correction without arguing for the mere fact that we might actually be in the wrong. Rather be wronged than being known as a self-righteous, never wrong, always right, can't be corrected, kind of a person. This value defines us as children of the Kingdom of God. May this heart attitude of penitence before God be carried out into every conversation and encounter, we have with others. It is a beautiful thing to observe in Believers when they carry in themselves a spirit of penitence. Always keep an open heart and mind to carefully assess your life in view of God's Word with a repentant heart.

# 4

## MEEKNESS

**Definition:**

Meekness is the consistent characteristic of gentle submissiveness. Meekness is to present oneself in every situation as one who lives under the rule and directive of another. Meekness is living in absolute self-surrender to the Will of God.

**Scripture:**

> Matthew 5:5 (NIV 1984) 5 Blessed are the meek, for they will inherit the earth.

> Matthew 5:5 (AMP) [5] "Blessed [inwardly peaceful, spiritually secure, worthy of respect] are the [b]gentle[the kind-hearted, the sweet-spirited, the self-controlled], for they will inherit the earth."

> Matthew 6:10, John 4:34, John 6:38, Isaiah 53:7

**Characteristic explained:**

Meekness is expressed in living with a spirit of submissiveness, for the sake of Christ. Resistance, in-submission, self-will, and sometimes rebellion express the opposite of meekness. Meekness is seen when we choose to rather be the least, or wronged, than fighting and resisting the wrong done to us. Christ was *"like a Lamb before the slaughter"* He did not open His mouth, or resisted the injustice done to Him. Meekness requires the absolute surrender of any form of entitlement. The strength of meekness is seen in its full reliance on the God who sees and will let justice be done in the end.

**Life Application:**

We are meek when we submit ourselves to the Will of God and to rather trust Him for a favorable outcome than to fight for what we believe to be right. Joseph is one of the greatest examples to us of a man who lived in absolute meekness, and entrusted himself to God regardless of the injustices done to him. We show meekness when we give expression to everything, we do that we will only do what the Lord would have us do and say. Moses is possibly another great example of someone who entrusted himself entirely to the Will and determination of the Lord, especially when God determined that he would not enter the Promised Land himself. Obliging himself to the Will of God entirely is possibly one of the greatest examples to us of being meek and submitting to the Will of God.

## 5

# SPIRITUAL PASSION

**Definition:**

Spiritual Passion is expressed when we give ourselves fully to our faith and His way of living. To have spiritual passion is to fully express oneself in what you belief and stand for.

**Scripture:**

> Matthew 5:6 (NIV 1984) 6 Blessed are those who
>     hunger and thirst for righteousness, for they will
>     be filled.

> 1 Timothy 4:12, 15; Romans 12:11.

**Characteristic explained:**

Words, which are sometimes associated with defining spiritual passion, are: eagerness, zeal, enthusiasm, excitement, spiritedness, fervency, fascination and obsession. To have spiritual passion is to be wholly sold out to what you belief and stand for. It is to be totally in love with the One you gave your life to. There should be no doubt to anyone who knows your Name that you are a Believer in Jesus Christ and that you are passionately pursuing Him and desire everything He has to offer. Spiritual passion is seen in the way in which we pursue Him and His Word, and the concurrent way in which we pursue the application of these values into our lives.

## Life Application:

Spiritual Passion characterizes those who through their words, actions and deeds show their hunger and thirst for more of God, and His Word. May our spiritual fervor and pursuit of Him, and growth in Him, be visible to everyone. Apollos, a Follower of Jesus, was such a man of whom we read in Acts 18 verse 25. The Apostle Paul exhibited such spiritual fervor as we read about his zeal in Colossians 1 verse 28. James 5 verse 16 speaks of the fervent prayers of a righteous man. It accomplishes a lot. May we be fervent in our faith and worship of God.

# 6

# MERCIFULNESS

**Definition:**

Mercy is the ability to consistently practice forbearance and leniency towards those who are failing and falling.

**Scripture:**

> Matthew 5:7 (NIV 1984) 7 Blessed are the merciful, for
>    they will be shown mercy.

> Luke 6:36, Deuteronomy 4:31, James 2:13.

**Characteristic explained:**

To be merciful is to be full of forbearance towards others as they face their shortcomings and failures. Words that best describe mercy are: compassion, pity, forgiveness, kindness and sympathy. Mercy is being generous in sympathy and expressed by a showing of caring and understanding. Mercy is being loving towards those in misery. Mercy is to possess a forgiving spirit toward those who sin against you. This virtue develops, out of our own personal experience of the mercy of God.

**Life Application:**

We are merciful when we fill ourselves with an understanding and forbearance towards others, that they might fail and fall. Mercy is best understood when we carefully consider how we desire God to deal with us, and treat us, when we come before Him with, knowing that he knows our every thought, action and word. We desire God to be gracious, compassionate, understanding and forgiving when we've messed up. May we find the Grace of God welled up in us to such an extent that we might deal with others in that same gracious and compassionate way. May we deal with the failures and shortcomings of others in a sympathetic and caringly understanding way. This is being merciful. Mercy is shown when we are being *a Good Samaritan.* (Luke 10:25-37) *Jesus forgave those who crucified Him.* (Luke 23:34) *Stephen forgave those who stoned him.* (Acts 7:60) In the "Our Father" Jesus spoke about forgiving those who sinned against us. Be Merciful.

# 7

# PURITY

**Definition:**

Purity is characterised by freedom from immorality, adultery and sinful contamination, and is a value of the Kingdom of God.

**Scripture:**

> Matthew 5:8 (NIV 1984) 8 Blessed are the pure in heart,
>    for they will see God.

> Psalms 24:3-5, Philippians 4:8,
> 1 Timothy 1:5, 2 Timothy 2:20, and 1 Timothy 4:12.

**Characteristic explained:**

Purity is associated with cleanness, wholesomeness, moral goodness, piety, uprightness, decency, worthiness, innocence, chastity and virtue. Purity is the result of living truthfully to God and yourself. Purity is the state of thought in which we are uncorrupted by worldly pleasures or passions. Fearing God, and living according to His Word, keeps our hearts pure. (Psalms 19:9, 119:9.) Our thoughts ultimately determine how we value purity. Our thoughts determine the seat chastity will have in our hearts.

## Life Application:

Purity is seen in us by what we observe, speak about, and allow access into our lives through our senses. In other words, when people visit your house they will quickly see how pure and uncontainable you keep your life by seeing what television programs you watch, the books you have in your house, the movies you watch, the stories you tell and the things which drives your passion. We need to ensure that the channels, through which we feed our mind, and ultimately our hearts, need to be clean and uncontaminated. Whatever we feed our senses with is what we fill our thoughts with. Psalms 15 verse 26 encourages us to have thoughts that are pleasing to the Lord. You see, so often people are judged by what they do, but in reality, the body follows where the mind went first, and once the mind digested evil and wrong paths, the body follows. I pray that we will be those who will pursue purity in our minds and protect our hearts from being corrupted with the things of the world.

Purity is also an outflow of the sanctifying work of the Holy Spirit. As we allow His cleansing and purifying work to continue in our lives, we become the men and woman God desired us to be – Pure.

# 8

# PEACEMAKERS

**Definition:**

A peacemaker is someone who steps up in every adversarial situation to bring peace. Peacemakers are reconciliatory in action.

**Scripture:**

> Matthew 5:9 (NIV 1984) 9 Blessed are the peacemakers,
>       for they will be called sons of God.

> James 3:18, Romans 14:19, Romans 12:18, Psalms 34:14,
>       Acts 7:26, 2 Corinthians 5:19-20, Ephesians 4:3.

**Characteristic explained:**

Being a peacemaker is being someone who seeks to bring adversaries together and to earnestly seek to establish reconciliation between them. Words that are strongly associated with peacemaking are: mediator, arbitrator, appeaser, diplomat, conciliator, negotiator, or pacifier. In one sense, this is what God calls us to be, when among those who are at odds with each other. Just think about the profile of a diplomat. Just think about someone who is engaged in arbitrating a hostile situation. Think about the characteristics of someone who is mediating a suitable, and agreeable outcome between two opposing parties. In that picture lies our calling. This is what God calls each one of us to practice as a peacemaker.

## Life Application:

It is hard to help others to be reconciled if you are still struggling in your own life. A Peacemaker first needs to have peace in his/her own heart, having been reconciled with God, before he/she could help others to be reconciled with God and fellow man. Being a Peacemaker is being committed to helping people, as far as what is possible, to live at peace with each other. It is so easy to shrug your shoulders, and dismiss yourself out of a difficult situation, where people beg you for your input, but this is exactly the moment to which we are called to step up and apply ourselves as peacemakers.

# PART III

## ASSIMILATION SHEET

### Spiritual Discipline

1. What is the first Scripture, we read of, that Jesus used to teach His Disciples on the Discipline of prayer? _____

_____

2. What is the first prayer Jesus taught His Disciples and where do you find it in Scripture? _____

_____

3. Name the various places of significance in the Tabernacle prayer?

_____

_____

_____

_____

. . .

4. Name one of the articles in the Ark of the Covenant and explain the significance of it to us? _____

_____

_____

_____

**Kingdom Values**

5. What is the first Value Jesus taught His Disciples? _____

_____

6. Why is humility such a huge value in the Kingdom of God?

_____

_____

_____

7. Describe Mournfulness in your own word.

_____

_____

_____

8. Why is purity such a huge value in the Kingdom of God?

_____

_____

_____

8. Which other Value do you want to embrace more, and why?

_____

_____

_____

_____

# WEEK THREE

# PART I

## SPIRITUAL DISCIPLINE: READING, MEDITATING AND PRACTICING THE WORD OF GOD

# READING, MEDITATING AND PRACTICING THE WORD OF GOD.

Jesus taught us *the Spiritual Discipline of having an intake of the Word of God* on a Daily Basis. During His days of Testing, Jesus used the Word to defend and persevere through the temptations Satan tried on Him. Jesus quoted Deuteronomy 8 verse 3 that: *"Man shall not live by bread alone, but by every Word that proceeds from the mouth of God."* Jesus presented Himself as the Bread of Life. Every New Testament Book endorses and encourages us to embrace the Words of the Lord on a daily basis.

> Luke 4:4 (NKJV) "4 But Jesus answered him, saying, "It is written, 'Man shall not live by bread alone, but by every word of God.'"

> Psalms 1:1-3 NIV "1 Blessed is the one who does not walk in step with the wicked or stand in the way that sinners take or sit in the company of mockers, 2 but whose delight is in the law of the Lord, and who meditates on his Law Day and night. 3 That person is like a tree planted by streams of water,

which yields its fruit in season and whose leaf does
not wither— whatever they do prospers."

Colossians 3:16 NIV "16 Let the Word of Christ dwell
among you richly as you teach and admonish one
another with all wisdom through psalms, hymns,
and songs from the Spirit, singing to God with
gratitude in your hearts."

Romans 10:17 ESV "17 So faith comes from hearing,
and hearing through the word of Christ."

The effectiveness in assimilating and treasuring the Word of God
is determined by the heart attitude with which we take time in the
Word of God, as well as our willingness and determination to put it
into practice.

The Fruitfulness and success of our growth in the Lord, and our
Faith in Him, firmly relies on our embracing of the Bible as God's
irrevocable Word to us, and the Foundation upon which we will
build our Faith.

### What is the Bible?

The Bible is the inerrant Word of God. The Bible is the most
reputable book ever written. The Bible was written over a 1500-year
period by over 40 Authors who wrote Messages from God down as
the Holy Spirit inspired them.

The Bible was compiled over a period of time and determined to
be the Holy Scriptures. The First Canon of Scriptures was the
Hebrew Bible and it consisted of the Old Testament writings as we
know it today.

## The Hebrew Bible

The Hebrew Bible is known as the Tanakh[1], which consist of three parts. The First Part consisted of the first five Books of the Bible and was known as the Torah. The second compilation was known as the Nevi'im[2] and consisted of the *"Former Prophets"*, the books of Joshua, Judges, Samuel and Kings, and the Prophetic books of Isaiah, Jeremiah and Ezekiel and the Twelve Minor Prophets. The third part consisted of the Ketuvim[3] which consisted of Psalms, Proverbs and Job, then also the "Hamesh Migillot" which consisted of Lamentations, Esther, Song of Songs, Ruth, Ecclesiastes and the remaining Books of Daniel, Ezra-Nehemiah and the Chronicles.[4] The Tanakh was accepted as "Holy Scriptures" by the 2 B.C.[5]

## The Septuagint

The Septuagint is the first translation of the Tanakh into Greek.

## The New Testament

The New Testament is a collection of 27 books consisting of 4 parts; namely the Four Gospels, the Acts of the Apostles, the Pastoral Epistles and an Apocalyptic Prophetic Book.[6] These books that were canonized as Sacred Writings was all written between 50 – 120 AD,[7] and affirmed through the determination at various gatherings of Church Leaders. As early as 382 at the Council of Rome[8] the incorporation of these 27 books was accepted as part of the complete Bible.

### The Authority of the Bible

The Authority of the Bible can be argued from an Archeological, Historical, and Prophetic dimension. It is more than coincidence that people without Internet, social media or postal services could speak so accurately into future events, which was fulfilled, unless it was Divinely inspired.

The Dead Sea Scrolls, amongst other historical manuscripts, support the accuracy of the writings and the inerrancy of the Scriptures. The Authority of the Scriptures was determined by the consistency of its Message through so many writers, over so many years, from so many varied backgrounds. They all had the same message and as "their" messages came into fulfillment, their cohesive and divinely ordered origin was affirmed. We often speak about the best Wisdom coming from seeing things in hindsight. The more manuscripts are discovered the more it affirms the miracle of having the "Words of God" in written memory.

We therefor build our lives on the Bible as the inerrant Word of God. I encourage you to hold your Bible in high regard. Treasure its contents as it holds the keys to life eternal.

How can I make the most of developing this Discipline of Reading, Meditating and practicing the Word of God?

## Make a daily commitment

A Good discipline in assimilating the Word of God is to:

- Make a commitment to do it daily.
- Set aside a specific and dedicated time to be alone with God and in His Word.
- Find and follow a Bible Reading plan. It will help you read through the entire Bible on a yearly basis.
- Get a Year Bible. I have seen this being used by my wife for over 30 years. It works!
- Whilst reading the Bible daily, apply the SOAP method to ensure that you don' just read the Bible as if it is another book, but as it really is: God's Word to you and me to live by.

## Use the SOAP method

- SOAP stands for:
- S – _____ (The specific reading of the day),
- O – **Observation** (What is God saying to me through the reading of today?),
- A – _____ (How can I put this into practice today? How can I do this? And make a commitment to do it), and
- P – **Prayer** (Pray that application into your life. Eg, God, today you spoke to me about forgiveness through Your Word. I choose to forgive like you want me to. I commit to forgive those who are going to do things that I don't like. I forgive them. I forgive those who are harmful and hurtful towards me. Help me to be quick to forgive. Thank you for your forgiveness. Amen.)

## Listen and do!

Encounter God through your daily reading of the Bible. God speaks, and desires to speak to us as His children. Listen and do! You will always be encouraged and strengthened through the reading and meditation of the Word.

## Meditate on the Word

Meditate on the Word of God. Pause, while reading, and think about it. Learn the Word of God.

## Study the Bible.

Take those Scriptures that stand out to you, and those that you sense God is speaking to you about, and learn them, meditate on them, and remind God about His promises to you regularly.

∽

**Be a man and woman of the Word of God.**

**Where do you start?**

Start by reading the Gospel of John. Read at least three chapters of the New and Old Testament a day. Also read 5 Psalms and 1 chapter in Proverbs. This will put you on a good and healthy spiritual discipline diet.

# PART II

## VALUES OF THE KINGDOM OF GOD

## 2

# PATIENT ENDURANCE UNDER SUFFERING

**Definition:**

*Patient endurance under suffering is the ability to endure through unjust treatment because of your faith.* It is to go beyond the expected response to such attacks by acting in a non-retaliatory way.

**Scripture:**

> Matthew 5:10-12 (NIV) [10] *Blessed are those who are persecuted because of righteousness,* for theirs is the kingdom of heaven. [11] *"Blessed are you when people insult you, persecute you and falsely say all kinds of evil against you because of me.* [12] Rejoice and be glad, because *great is your reward in heaven,* for in the same way they persecuted the prophets who were before you.

> Luke 6:22 (NIV), 1 Peter 2:19-20 (NIV), Matthew 5:38-42 (NIV), Matthew 16:24 (NIV)

**Characteristic explained:**

When Christ gave us the promise of the empowerment of the Holy Spirit in Acts 1 verse 8, He said that the Power of the Holy Spirit was for us to be His Witnesses. That word "**witnesses**" is the Greek word "**Martus**" which is akin to "**Martur**" from which we derived our English word "**martyr.**" In essence, to be a witness is to approach everyday with the preparedness that you might be persecuted, slandered, receive unjust treatment, martyred, because of your allegiance and alignment with Christ. This value further defines us as children of God, of the Kingdom of Heaven. Jesus said that those who endure such treatment are blessed, and will receive a great reward in Heaven.

**Life Application:**

The life application of this characteristic really requires us to "*turn the other cheek*" and to "*walk the second mile.*" We give full expression to this value when we willingly live a life of self-denial for the sake of Christ.

## 3

# EXAMPLE

**Definition:**

*Being an example is the expression we give as to how much we value the Lord Jesus*, and *the extent to which we desire to make His Name known* among the people of the earth.

**Scripture:**

> Matthew 5:13-16 (NIV) Salt and Light 13 *"You are the salt of the earth.* But if the salt loses its saltiness, how can it be made salty again? It is no longer good for anything, except to be thrown out and trampled by men. 14 *"You are the light of the world.* A city on a hill cannot be hidden. 15 Neither do people light a lamp and put it under a bowl. Instead they put it on its stand, and it gives light to everyone in the house. 16 In the same way, *let your light shine before men, that they may see your good deeds and praise your Father in heaven."*

Matthew 12:34-37 (NIV), 1 Timothy 4:12 (NIV), 1
Corinthians 11:1 (NIV)

## Characteristic explained:

Being an example is an inner awareness and aptitude to present
oneself as an example to follow, which is visible through one's
behaviour, actions and words.

## Life Application:

Being an example is an intentional awareness that God made me a
light to shine in such a way that it will bring and point people to
Christ. Valuing being an Example is attending to one's conduct, and
presenting oneself in the highest stature possible, at all times.

## 4

# CUSTODIAN

**Definition:**

*A custodian is a keeper, preserver and defender of the Word of God and seeks in earnest to uphold the Word of God in every situation and circumstance.* A Custodian is an upholder, practitioner and advocate for the moral guidelines God set for His people.

**Scripture:**

> Matthew 5:19 (NIV) "19 Anyone who breaks one of the least of these commandments and teaches others to do the same will be called least in the kingdom of heaven, but *whoever practices and teaches these commands will be called great in the kingdom of heaven.*"

> Mark 12:29-31 (NIV), John 15:14 (NIV)

**Characteristic explained:**

To be a custodian is to keep something sacred and secured by intentional practice. To be a Custodian is to be a Law keeper. To be a custodian is to be a preserver of something that's of high value. Custodians are those people who live to keep valuable customs and principles, especially for future generations to observe. They are the protectors and good stewards of passing on the values and principles taught or passed on to them. A custodian is also one who guards and defends something of high value, from outside interference and influence.

**Life Application:**

From Jesus' teaching we learn that practicing and teaching people to obey the commandments of the Lord, is highly valued. We value being custodians when we both practice the observance of the Ten Commandments, as well as teach others to practice and obey it as well. As custodians of the commands of the Lord we firstly practice these commands in our own lives. The biggest impact we can ever make is by holding the commands of the Lord in observance in our own lives. When we keep these commands, we maintain the use of it, and thereby ensuring its future use.

# 5

# RECONCILIATORY

**Definition:**

To be reconciliatory is to be a proactive initiator to restore relation-ships and defuse conflicts. We value reconciliation when we take the initiative to sort things out with a brother or sister, and this is what Jesus encourages us to do.

**Scripture:**

> Matthew 5:23-24 (NIV) 23 "Therefore, **if you** are
> offering your gift **at the altar** and **there remember**
> **that your brother has something against you,** 24
> leave your gift there in front of the altar. **First go**
> **and be reconciled to your brother;** then come and
> offer your gift.
>
> Matthew 18:15-17 (NIV), 2 Corinthians 5:18-20 (NIV)

**Characteristic explained:**

Being a reconciler is being someone who desires and works towards restoring friendly relations between people. This applies to yourself when other people are upset with you, or have something against you, or with you assisting others to be reconciled, who have unsettled feuds between them. Reconciliation means that they settle their disputes appropriately and work together in unity and harmony going forward. Reconciliation requires humility, forgiveness, mercy and grace.

**Life Application:**

Many people have unsettled feuds. In humility, and in consistent pursuit of the instruction of the Lord to live at peace with all men, let us help our Brothers in their broken relationships.

# 6

# RESOLUTENESS

**Definition:**

Resoluteness describes the value of being a man or woman of your word, even if it hurts.

**Scripture:**

> Matthew 5:37 (NIV) 37 Simply **let your 'Yes' be 'Yes,'** and your 'No,' 'No'; anything beyond this comes from the evil one.

> Matthew 5:33 (NIV), Psalms 15:4 (NIV), Deuteronomy 23:21 (NIV), Joshua 24:15 (KJV)

**Characteristic explained:**

To be resolute is to make decisions firmly, purposefully, quickly and with determination. To be resolute is to make determined decisions. To be resolute is to not allow anything to get in the way of the decision you made. It is to be a man or woman of your word, and to stand by what you agreed, even if it hurts you. A resolute person is one that is solid, sound, firm, determined and unwavering to the oath or promise they made.

**Life Application:**

I grew up in South Africa, and I grew up on this value. We have a saying: "My Word is my Bond." It simply means that if I have given you my Word, it is as good as giving you a Bank Guaranteed Cheque. Resolute people are unwavering in their convictions and decisive in fulfilling their word. Be a person of your word.

# 7

# LOVING

**Definition:**

Love is a strong feeling of affection and endearment.

**Scriptures:**

> Matthew 5:43-48 (NIV) "43 "You have heard that it was said, 'Love your neighbor and hate your enemy.' 44 But I tell you: **Love your enemies and pray for those who persecute you, 45 that you may be sons of your Father in heaven.** He causes his sun to rise on the evil and the good, and sends rain on the righteous and the unrighteous. 46 If you love those who love you, what reward will you get? Are not even the tax collectors doing that? 47 And if you greet only your brothers, what are you doing more than others? Do not even pagans do that? 48 **Be perfect, therefore, as your heavenly Father is perfect.**"

John 13:34 -35 (NIV), 1 John 4:7-8 (NIV), 1 John 4:12
(NIV), Romans 12:10 (NIV)

## Characteristic explained:

Love can be explained by words such as affection, adoration, deep friendship, tenderness, fondness, amity and devotion. Love is that expression of tender affection towards somebody. Love is the affection you show when you like something or someone very much. Love is also when you feel a desire for somebody. Love is defined by a passionate attraction and desire towards someone. A strong liking and an accompanying friendly and kind enthusiasm express love.

## Life Application:

We value loving when we give expression of our thoughts, through our heartfelt actions, to show and express endearment, adoration, affection, fondness and deep friendship. We value love when we unconditionally show our affection in meaningful ways. All people have a need and a desire to be loved. Love is from God. Love God, love His people, love the Samaritans, and those who hurt, abused and rejected you. Love God's Commandments with all your heart. We show that we love God by the way we obey His commandments. Say to someone today: *"I love you!"* and mean it. Love drives away fear. Love unifies. There is power in love!

# 8

# DISCREETNESS

**Definition:**

Discreetness is the inherent value of doing extra-ordinary things without desiring to be seen or even acknowledged for doing them, except as unto the Lord.

**Scripture:**

> Matthew 6:3-4 (NIV) 3 But when you give to the needy, *do not let your left hand know what your right hand is doing*, 4 so that your giving may be in secret. Then your Father, who sees what is done in secret, will reward you.
>
> Matthew 6:6 (NIV), Matthew 6:17-18 (NIV), Colossians 3:23-24 (NIV)

**Characteristic explained:**

Discreetness is to deeply value doing things to honour God, and not man. To be discreet is to do things in an inconspicuous, unnoticeable, and modest way. It is the value of doing things in secret. Discreetness is also to practice retrain. It is to choose to rather understate achievements or things, than overstating them. It is the opposite of boastfulness.

**Life Application:**

I think that the Biblical teaching provide us with quite a significant example to follow. For us as Believers, we are sometimes called upon to exercise our faith in extra-ordinary ways, such as fasting. It is not the norm for people to fast, not even too fast for extended periods of time, however, for those of us who fast this is a value to embrace. As we observe the commands and leading of the Lord to give or fast for a cause, we need to take special caution to do so discreetly. May the rewards from above, on our lives and ministry, tell that we pray. If indeed we do everything to honour God, then discreetness should be an easy value to embrace.

# PART III

## ASSIMILATION SHEET

**Spiritual Discipline: Reading, meditating and practising the Word of God**

1. Complete the sentence. "Man shall not live by bread alone, but by every _____ of God.'"

2. Complete the acronym SOAP below, and explain each one.

S - _____- Reciting the Scripture that had the most impact on you during your daily reading.

O - _____- What do I sense God is speaking to me about in this Scripture.

A - _____- I commit to act on God's Word by doing the following.

P - _____- Ask God to help you in building this value into your life.

. . .

2. Which strategy will you follow to daily read and meditate on God's Word? _____

_____

## Values of the Kingdom of God

3. One of the Values is to be an "EXAMPLE." Why is this important to you? _____

_____

_____

_____

_____

4. What does it mean to be a Custodian? _____

_____

_____

_____

5. What does it mean to be resolute?_____

_____

_____

_____

_____

6. How can you be more considerate? _____

_____

_____

_____

_____

# WEEK FOUR

# PART I

## SPIRITUAL DISCIPLINE: FASTING

## 1

# FASTING

Jesus taught us on *the Spiritual Discipline of Fasting* in Matthew 6 verses 16-17. Jesus fasted 40 days prior to His earthly ministry started. We've upheld this practice of Fasting at the beginning of every year, for many years now.

> Matthew 6:16-17 (NIV) 16 "When you fast, do not look
> somber as the hypocrites do, for they disfigure
> their faces to show others they are fasting. Truly I
> tell you, they have received their reward in full. 17
> But when you fast, put oil on your head and wash
> your face,"

Jesus did not dismiss the challenge of the Pharisees when they questioned Him on the non-Fasting of His Disciples. He confirmed that they will be fasting when He is not with them any longer.

## Different types of fasting

The Bible basically describes three major types of fasting:

- A _____ Fast - A regular fast means that you refrain from eating all food, however, you still drink water or juice during a your fast. Jesus went on such a fast after His Baptism in the Jordan.

   Matthew 4:2 (NIV) "2 After fasting forty days and forty nights, he was hungry."

- A _____ Fast - This type of fast generally refers to omitting or refraining from certain types of foods. I think that Daniel defines this kind of fasting quite simply.

*Daniel 10:2-3 says, "At that time I, Daniel, mourned for three weeks. I ate no choice food; no meat or wine touched my lips; and I used no lotions at all until the three weeks were over".*

   Daniel 1:12 "Please test your servants for ten days: Give us nothing but vegetables to eat and water to drink."

- A _____ Fast - These fasts are complete fasts where you eat no food and drink no fluids. Paul went on a full fast for three days following his encounter with Jesus on the road to Damascus. Esther also asked Mordecai to call the Jews to a full fast for three days. It is recommended that this type of fast be done with extreme caution and not for extended periods of time.

   Acts 9:9 (NIV) ""For three days he was blind, and did not eat or drink anything."

Esther 4:15-16: "Then Esther sent this reply to
Mordecai: 'Go, gather together all the Jews who are
in Susa, and fast for me. Do not eat or drink for
three days, night or day. I and my maids will fast as
you do. When this is done, I will go to the king,
even though it is against the law. And if I perish, I
perish.'"

### Why do we fast?

Fasting is a Spiritual Discipline. We see many miracles and break-throughs occurred during times of fasting and prayer. The Bible is full of references to fasting by heroes such as Moses, Daniel, Esther, David, Ezra and many others. Jesus fasted for 40 days before embarking on His earthly ministry. The Church in Antioch fasted before commissioning Paul and Barnabas for their mission.

Great Revivalists, such as John Calvin, John Knox, John Wesley, and Martin Luther, all fasted. During a visit to Charlotte, NC, I learnt that Billy Graham fasted and prayed often during the years in which he produced some of the greatest revivals of our time.

Fasting is not: a way to manipulate God.

Fasting is: a means by which we confess our sins, turn from our wicked ways and turn to God. One of the many things we learn from the Biblical example on fasting and prayer is that it was always accompanied with confession of sins, repentance and a turning back towards God.

Fasting requires us to be attentive towards God with all of our hearts.

## Examples

There are many examples in the Word of God on prayer and fasting.

～

## Jesus taught on fasting

Jesus taught His disciples about fasting.

> Matthew 6:16-18 (NIV) "When you fast, do not look
> somber as the hypocrites do. For they disfigure
> their faces to show men they are fasting. I tell you
> the truth, they have received their reward in full.
> But when you fast, put oil on your head and wash
> your face, so that it will not be obvious to men that
> you are fasting..."

> Matthew 9:14-15 (NIV) "[14] Then John's disciples came
> and asked him, "How is it that we and the
> Pharisees fast often, but your disciples do not fast?"
> [15] Jesus answered, "How can the guests of the
> bridegroom mourn while he is with them? The
> time will come when the bridegroom will be taken
> from them; then they will fast."

**Jesus fasted prior to Him starting His earthly ministry.**

> Matthew 4:2 (NIV) "2 After fasting forty days and forty
> nights, he was hungry."

**Moses fasted at least twice for a period of 40 days.**

During the first time Moses fasted 40 days and 40 nights, He was called into the Cloud onto the Mountain of God. He was with God for 40 days while the Lord God wrote the Commandments of the Lord with His own finger on stones. During the second period of fasting, Moses wrote the words of the Covenant on tables of stone. These were two absolute divine times of fasting and produced things of eternal value.

Deuteronomy 9:9-10 (NIV) "9 When I went up on the
mountain to receive the tablets of stone, the tablets
of the covenant that the Lord had made with you, I
stayed on the mountain forty days and forty nights;
I ate no bread and drank no water. [10] The Lord gave
me two stone tablets inscribed by the finger of
God. On them were all the commandments
the Lord proclaimed to you on the mountain out of
the fire, on the day of the assembly."

Exodus 24:27-28 (NIV) "[27] Then the Lord said to Moses,
"Write down these words, for in accordance with
these words I have made a covenant with you and
with Israel." [28] Moses was there with the Lord forty
days and forty nights without eating bread or
drinking water. And he wrote on the tablets the
words of the covenant—the Ten Commandments.

### David fasted

David fasted regularly from some of his accounts in the Psalms.

Psalms 35:13 (NIV) "[13] Yet when they were ill, I put on
sackcloth and humbled myself with fasting. When
my prayers returned to me unanswered, [14] I went
about mourning as though for my friend or
brother. I bowed my head in grief as though
weeping for my mother."

### Ezra called for a fast for safety

Ezra 8:21 (NIV) "There, by the Ahava Canal, I [Ezra]
proclaimed a fast, so that we might humble
ourselves before our God and ask him for a safe

journey for us and our children, with all our possessions"

## Nehemiah called the Israelites to fasting

Nehemiah called the Israelites to fasting in the process of rebuilding the wall of Jerusalem.

> Nehemiah 9:1-3 (NIV) "[1] On the twenty-fourth day of the same month, the Israelites gathered together, fasting and wearing sackcloth and putting dust on their heads. [2] Those of Israelite descent had separated themselves from all foreigners. They stood in their places and confessed their sins and the sins of their ancestors. [3] They stood where they were and read from the Book of the Law of the Lord their God for a quarter of the day, and spent another quarter in confession and in worshiping the Lord their God."

## Esther and Mordecai called for a national fast

> Esther 4:15-16 (NIV) "[15] Then Esther sent this reply to Mordecai: [16] "Go, gather together all the Jews who are in Susa, and fast for me. Do not eat or drink for three days, night or day. I and my attendants will fast as you do. When this is done, I will go to the king, even though it is against the law. And if I perish, I perish."

## Joel called for Fasting and Prayer

*Fasting preceded the Prophetic Promise* of the Outpouring of the Holy Spirit.

God spoke to the Prophet Joel and he called the Nation to a Day of Fasting. His call for a National fast was accompanied with a Call for penitent prayers. It was only the "renting of the hearts" that would avert the fury of God. As the people repented and turned back to God and His ways, He relented and gave them the amazing and well-known promise of the outpouring of the Holy Spirit in the Last days.

> Joel 1:14 (AMP) "14 Consecrate a fast, Proclaim a
> solemn assembly, Gather the elders and all the
> inhabitants of the land To the house of
> the Lord your God, And cry out to the Lord [in
> penitent pleadings].

### Daniel Fasted

Daniel fasted and God heard his prayers, answered him and gave him tremendous insight, understanding and spiritual foresight and wisdom.

> Daniel 9:3-6 (NIV) "3 So I turned to the Lord God and
> pleaded with him in prayer and petition, in
> fasting, and in sackcloth and ashes. 4 I prayed to
> the Lord my God and confessed: "Lord, the great
> and awesome God, who keeps his covenant of
> love with those who love him and keep his
> commandments, 5 we have sinned and done
> wrong. We have been wicked and have rebelled; we
> have turned away from your commands and
> laws. 6 We have not listened to your servants the
> prophets, who spoke in your name to our kings,
> our princes and our ancestors, and to all the people
> of the land."

### Insight and understanding come through Fasting and Prayer

While Daniel was still fasting, God sent His Angel with a message and with insight and understanding. Read the entire chapter for deeper appreciation.

> Daniel 9:21-23 (NIV) "21 while I was still in prayer,
> Gabriel, the man I had seen in the earlier vision,
> came to me in swift flight about the time of the
> evening sacrifice. 22 He instructed me and said to
> me, "Daniel, I have now come to give you insight
> and understanding. 23 As soon as you began to
> pray, a word went out, which I have come to tell
> you, for you are highly esteemed. Therefore,
> consider the word and understand the vision:"

The moment we start to fast and pray, God engages the process of helping, guiding, answering and directing. I want to encourage you to Fast and pray regularly.

There are many examples on Fasting and prayer throughout the Bible. I am sure the Lord will use this seed in your spiritual development to grow and develop you into a mightily used man and woman of God.

### Samuel fasted in an act of repentance

> I Samuel 7:6 (NIV) "When they had assembled at
> Mizpah, they drew water and poured it out before
> the LORD. On that day they fasted and there they
> confessed, "We have sinned against the LORD."
> And Samuel was leader of Israel at Mizpah"

Isaiah gives us that wonderful Chapter 58, which is devoted to Fasting. Jeremiah recites fasting as part of the disciplines that was practiced by the people of Israel in Jeremiah 36.

## The Church in Antioch fasted and prayer before commissioning Paul and Barnabas

> Acts 13:2-3; 14:23(NIV) "While they were worshiping the
> Lord and fasting, the Holy Spirit said, 'Set apart for
> me Barnabas and Saul for the work to which I have
> called them.' So after they had fasted and prayed,
> they placed their hands on them and sent them
> off..."

> Acts 14:23 (NIV) "Paul and Barnabas appointed elders
> for them in each church and, with prayer and
> fasting, committed them to the Lord, in whom they
> had put their trust."

### Fasting is a Form of Worship

The prophetess, Anna, as part of her worship of God in the Temple, fasted and prayed.

> Luke 2:36-37 (NIV) "[36] There was also a prophet, Anna,
> the daughter of Penuel, of the tribe of Asher. She
> was very old; she had lived with her husband seven
> years after her marriage,[37] and then was a widow
> until she was eighty-four She never left the temple
> but worshiped night and day, fasting and praying."

### Some practical advice

I've found that the first few days are always the hardest. The typical obstacles you will face are physical, mental and spiritual in kind. Physically, you might experience headaches, depending on how well you detoxed prior to your period of fasting and prayer. You might experience body, muscle, and hunger pains. Try to counter this by drinking heaps of water, it will definitely help you get through the worst of it. Avoid drinking medicines during regular and full fasts, if possible. Medication will adversely affect your digestive and renal system.

One of your biggest challenges will be the Mental Challenge. During the first few days of a long fast you will find that there is the constant questioning this route to gain what you are trusting God for. The enemy is strongly at work during this time to keep you from continuing since he knows that you will gain power over all the power of the enemy through your fasting and prayer.

My best initial advice here is to *get a Mentor to guide and walk alongside you* when you do an extended fast. He will serve as a sound Soundboard and will help you through the onslaught on your mind, soul and body. Be sure to find an experienced mentor.

### Afterword

Remember, when we fast we engage in a sense into a spiritual warfare and sometimes, because of the weakness we experience with our fasting, we battle to discern between what is real and what is spiritual. It is only once you've broken through this barrier that you find yourself discerning with clarity and focus. Through Fasting and prayer our spiritual sense and alertness becomes more defined and sensitive, but remember, it was at the end of 40 days that Satan came to tempt Jesus. Be alert for his seduction and tricks to steal away from you the joy and harvest and accomplishment for what you are fasting. May the Lord be with you during this period of Fasting and prayer.

# PART II

## VALUES OF THE KINGDOM OF GOD

# 2

## FORGIVING

**Definition:**

*Forgiveness is the ability to permanently release those who wronged you,* and treat the offenders as if they never did a thing to hurt or harm you.

**Scriptures:**

> Matthew 6:12 (NIV) 12 **Forgive us our debts, as we also have forgiven our debtors.**

> Matthew 6:14-15 (NIV), Colossians 3:13 (NIV), Matthew 18:21-22 (NIV)

**Characteristic explained:**

*Forgiveness is one of the strongest values on earth.* It holds the power to health and healing, but also to death and destruction. Forgiveness is defined by our ability to let go of an offence, hurt or wrong done to us. It is that constant act of pardoning others. It is the extending of compassionate grace to those who hurt us, abuse us, and cause pain to us. Forgiveness is defined by being merciful, understanding, tolerant, and pitiful. It is in the light of our dependency and appreciation on God's forgiveness that we liberally forgive. The key to receiving and being forgiven is in our hands.

**Life Application:**

We fill ourselves with grace and mercy to forgive every offence levelled against us every morning. What Jesus taught us was to forgive *"seventy-seven times a day."* If the yardstick of "seventy-seven times" is upheld in our lives, I believe we will be a very forgiving people and true examples of being followers of Jesus. Even under extreme circumstances do we find the example of Jesus and His Disciples bearing witness of this value in their lives. The words: "Father forgive them, for they do not know what they are doing," stand as a testimony and an example for us to follow. May we forgive often, willingly and freely. I am reminded of this value in my life every morning when I bow down to pray and recite the "Our Father." May this prayer, especially the *"and forgive us our trespasses as we forgive those who trespassed against us,"* find a permanent home in our actions and dealings with others every day. May our attitudes and actions bear witness of our heartfelt pardoning of others.

## 3

# KINGDOM OF GOD INVESTOR

**Definition:**

A Kingdom of God Investor is someone who values the Kingdom of God above earthly thing and as an expression of that value, puts their treasures into the Kingdom of God.

**Scripture:**

> Matthew 6:19-21 (NIV) Treasures in Heaven "19 "Do not
> store up for yourselves treasures on earth, where
> moth and rust destroy, and where thieves break in
> and steal. 20 But store up for yourselves treasures
> in heaven, where moth and rust do not destroy, and
> where thieves do not break in and steal. 21 For
> where your treasure is, there your heart will be
> also."

> Acts 2:44-45 (NIV), Acts 4:32 (NIV), 2 Corinthians 9:6

(NIV), 2 Corinthians 9:7-8 (NIV), 2 Corinthians
9:10-11 (NIV)

## Characteristic explained:

The Principle of sowing and reaping stand central in this value.
**Whatever we sow, we reap.** The best place to sow is in the Kingdom
of God. **The early Believers truly valued the Teachings of the Lord
Jesus by not storing for themselves treasures on earth.** Their treasures were sown into the Kingdom of God, and therefore, as the
Scriptures say: "there heart will be there also." It never ceases to
amaze me to see where people's hearts are, and how they value the
Kingdom of God in relation to how they treasure it with their treasures. Investments made into the work of God should reflect how we
value God's work, and how we value being entrusted with seed.

## Life Application:

To value the Kingdom of God is to treasure it. We treasure the
Kingdom of God when we place our proceeds with a willing and
cheerful heart into the Church.

**How do we do that?**

1. We honour God with a tithe (ten percent) of all our income;

2. We offer up to Him a sacrificial gift from the remaining ninety
percent of our income, just as we obediently and willingly present to
our Governments that part of our income as tax, as what they require
of us to give.

3. We sow into the Work of God by supporting Missionaries,
Orphanages, the destitute and the poor. The latter should be done in
secret and not done so that others could see.

# 4

## GOD-MINDED

**Definition:**

Being God-minded means that you think about God, His Word and the eternal things of above, all the time. It is a Kingdom value to be God-minded.

**Scripture:**

> Matthew 6:24 (NIV) 24 "No one can serve two masters.
> Either he will hate the one and love the other, or he
> will be devoted to the one and despise the other.
> **You cannot serve both God and Money.**

> Colossians 3:1-2 (NIV), Romans 8:5 (NIV), Psalms 1:2
> (NIV), Deuteronomy 6:4-9 (NIV)

**Characteristic explained:**

To be God-minded is to be single-minded on God, and the things of God. From the earliest dealings with man, God always expressed a desire and commanded that He should be at the centre of our thoughts, actions and deliberations. He encouraged His people to love Him with all of their hearts, mind and strength. He wanted His people to talk about Him all the time, and to make permanent reminders to carry with them. He also encouraged His people to write His commandments on the doorposts of their houses. To be God-minded is to take every effort and action to keep the Lord God at the forefront of our thought, action and speech.

**Life Application:**

How do we put this Kingdom Value into action in our lives? Well, a good way to do that is to start each day by reading and meditating on the Word of God, and to pray. When I was a child, we used to learn memory verses for school and Sunday school. This might be a good discipline to practice, now that we are older and our capacity much more increased, to learn one of the verses we read during our morning devotion and then to recite them to our families during our evening family devotion.

This way we will both meditate on the Word of God, and keep the Word of God at the forefront of our minds. Another, more permanent way might be to put meaningful Scriptures up on our walls as statement or art pieces, but also as declaration Scriptures. We live in an era in which we could put Scriptures up as a screensaver or as background pictures on our smart watches, smartphones, tablets and computers. The goal is not just to place outward signs, but also to create ways in which we can be more God-minded in our everyday life. I pray that you too will set up such signposts for your life to keep the Lord God at the centre of your life.

# KINGDOM OF GOD PRIORITIZER

**Definition:**

We know that we truly place the Kingdom of God as a high priority in our lives when we seek to put the Kingdom values above that of our own. We value the Kingdom of God when it takes precedence over every decision we make.

**Scriptures:**

> Matthew 6:33 (NIV) 33 But *seek first his kingdom and his righteousness*, and all these things will be given to you as well.

> 2 Chronicles 18:4 (NIV), Matthew 6:10-13 (NIV), Colossians 3:15 (AMPC)

**Characteristic explained:**

A Kingdom of God seeker prioritizes the Will of God over his or her own. To have this as a Value in one's life means that you seek guidance, approval, direction and favour from God prior to doing anything. It is that heartfelt submission to the Will of God in everything we do. Before we decide on anything, we seek what God wants us to do in regard to that matter. It requires the daily desire to walk in the perfect will of God.

**Life Application:**

We value being a Kingdom of God seeker when we intentionally seek God's approval, guidance, and instruction prior to doing anything. It is that daily enquiring of the Lord for His Will to be done. It is to submit every decision to God for His guidance and ultimate instruction. Peace plays a major part in knowing assuredly what the will of God is in any decision.

How do we do this? Submit your decisions to God in prayer, and then over coming days, as you read His Word, or listen to the inner voice of the Holy Spirit, find His guidance. You will always have a strong sense of peace when you've conceded to the Will of God.

## 6

# INTROSPECTIVE

**Definition:**

*Introspection is the constant self-awareness, and assessment of our own standing before God*, and thereby enabling us to be considered in our assessment of others' actions and deeds.

**Scriptures:**

> Matthew 7:1-2 (NIV) 1 **"Do not judge, or you too will be judged.** 2 For **in the same way you judge others, you will be judged**, and with the measure you use, it will be measured to you.
>
> Matthew 7:3-5 (NIV), John 8:7 (NIV)

**Characteristic explained:**

To value being introspective is valuing first assessing one's own life before passing comment or judgement on others. Introspection helps us make balanced assessments of other's actions. Being introspective is being thoughtful, reflective and considered in one's approach to others. It is the embracing of that self-examining, contemplative approach to everyday life.

**Life Application:**

The question that helps us being level-headed in every situation is always:

- *"If others had to assess me, in the matter of my concern or judgement, what would they say?"*

If there might even be the slightest chance that they would judge my actions, behaviour or manners in the same way, then maybe I should not be the one to pass judgement. Jesus demonstrated this with the woman who was caught in adultery. I wonder how much more gracious we would live towards others if we truly value introspection. May we always be introspective before passing comments or judgements on others.

## 7

# PERSISTENCE

**Definition:**

*Being persistent is living a life in full pursuit without giving up.* Keep on asking, seeking and knocking since we have this Promise. Persistence moves you to explore every possibility for an outcome.

**Scriptures:**

> Matthew 7:7-8 (NIV) "7 *"Ask* and it will be given to you; *seek* and you will find; *knock* and the door will be opened to you. 8 *For everyone who asks receives; he who seeks finds; and to him who knocks, the door will be opened.* "

> Luke 18:1 (NIV) The Parable of the Persistent Widow "1 Then *Jesus told his disciples* a parable to show them that *they should always pray and not give up.*"

**Characteristic explained:**

*Persistence is the value of being persevering, tenacious, enduring and unrelenting.* It is in inner aptitude of hope and faith that things will come through, things will turn out ok, that circumstances will change for good. Persistence is seen in the way one shows determination and obstinacy to not give in or give up. Through the Parable of the Persistent Woman, Jesus taught us this lesson of persistent pursuit of the things we believe in, and to trust the Lord to do things in our lives, without wavering.

**Life Application:**

We all have hopes and dreams, unfortunately many of us give up on our hopes and dreams as if they are unreachable. We apply this value in our lives when we start hoping and dreaming again. Start believing again that the impossible can become possible. When you trust God for something, don't give up on holding on to that Promise, that Scripture, or that Message from God. Hold on to promises of God like Joseph who believed God, and saw the fulfillment of God's Promise to him. He was persistent and saw the fulfillment of the dream God gave him. Be like an Abraham who believed God, even though he and his wife were as good as dead.

# CONSIDERATE

**Definition:**

*Consideration is the value of acting thoughtfully and with care, before-hand, as to how your preferences, actions, presence at certain places and responses, might impact others.*

**Scriptures:**

> Matthew 7:12 (NIV) 12 So in everything, *do to others*
> *what you would have them do to you,* for this sums
> up the Law and the Prophets.
> Philippians 2:4, Romans 14:13 (NIV)

**Characteristic explained:**

*Being considerate is being thoughtful, mindful, and careful about how one's actions and words might negatively impact others.* To be considerate is to be mindful, respectful, selfless and kind, especially as it relates to others. Consideration is applied when we consciously think about our actions, words and reactions beforehand. To be considerate is to be contemplative, understanding and sympathetic.

**Life Application:**

We are considerate when we act in a thoughtful and mindful way towards others. We are considerate when we honestly assess our reactions and responses. The question:

- *"Would I like others to treat me in the way in which I am about to treat someone else?"*

The answer to this question should answer and show us just how considerate we really are. So, on the one hand "Consideration" is the application and thoughtfulness over How our conduct, liberties and presence might negatively impact others, but then also how considered we are in treating people with the same kind of respect and courtesy as what we would love them to treat us.

# PART III

## ASSIMILATION SHEET

**Spiritual Discipline: Fasting**

1. Did Jesus teach His Disciples on Fasting? _____
   If Yes, What did Jesus teach His Disciples on Fasting?
   _____
   _____
   _____

2. What Kind of Fasts are taught in the Bible?
   _____
   _____
   3. How long did Moses Fast? _____
   4. How long did Daniel Fast? _____
   5. How long did Esther Fast? _____
   6. How long did Jesus Fast? _____

# Values of the Kingdom of God

7. *"Forgiving"* is a Kingdom Value. Why is Forgiving such an amazing Kingdom Value? _____

_____

_____

8. Where should we invest our resources?

_____

_____

9. How can you be more *"God-minded"*? _____

_____

_____

_____

10. What does it mean to be *"Introspective"*? _____

_____

_____

_____

11. How can you be more *"considerate"*? _____

_____

_____

12. What does it mean to be "persistent"? _____

_____

_____

# WEEK FIVE

# PART I

## SPIRITUAL DISCIPLINE - STEWARDSHIP

# 1

## STEWARDSHIP

Jesus taught us on *the Spiritual Discipline of Stewardship* in Matthew 6 verses 2-4, and through the Parable of the Talents in Matthew 25 verses 14 -30. On one occasion He taught them that good stewardship is to pay their taxes in Matthew 22 verses 15 to 22. These are of course just a snippet of an in-depth study on Stewardship.

> Matthew 6:3-4 (NIV) "3 But when you give to the needy, do not let your left hand know what your right hand is doing, 4 so that your giving may be in secret. Then your Father, who sees what is done in secret, will reward you."

### Stewardship is an act of generosity

Stewardship is first and foremost an act of generosity towards God. It is our way of honouring God, returning to Him what belongs to Him, and giving freely as He guides and directs us.

Good stewardship requires generosity. The Apostle Paul was teaching the Corinthian Church on how generous the Macedonians were towards him and his ministry. When we sow, we need to sow into good soil. The work of God is the best soil you could ever invest your finances in.

> 2 Corinthians 9:6-15 Sowing Generously
> "[6] Remember this: Whoever sows sparingly will also reap sparingly, and whoever sows generously will also reap generously. [7] Each man should give what he has decided in his heart to give, not reluctantly or under compulsion, for God loves a cheerful giver. [8] And God is able to make all grace abound to you, so that in all things at all times, having all that you need, you will abound in every good work. [9] As it is written: "He has scattered abroad his gifts to the poor; his righteousness endures forever." [10] Now he who supplies seed to the sower and bread for food will also supply and increase your store of seed and will enlarge the harvest of your righteousness. [11] You will be made rich in every way so that you can be generous on every occasion, and through us your generosity will result in thanksgiving to God. [12] This service that you perform is not only supplying the needs of God's people but is also overflowing in many expressions of thanks to God. [13] Because of the service by which you have proved yourselves, men will praise God for the obedience that accompanies your confession of the gospel of Christ, and for your generosity in sharing with them and with everyone else. [14] And in their prayers for you their hearts will go out to you, because of the surpassing grace God has given you. [15] Thanks be to God for his indescribable gift!"

May we be good stewards in the generous way in which we give to God, and His work.

## Stewardship is about Accountability

Stewardship is also about us taking responsibility for the talents, gifts and blessings we have received from God, and then administer good care over the entrustments to us. Jesus explained this Kingdom value through a Parable.

> Matthew 25:14, 20-21 (NKJV) The Parable of the Talents
> "14 "For the kingdom of heaven is like a man traveling to a far country, who called his own servants and delivered his goods to them." 20 "So he who had received five talents came and brought five other talents, saying, 'Lord, you delivered to me five talents; look, I have gained five more talents besides them.' 21 His lord said to him, 'Well done, good and faithful servant; you were faithful over a few things, I will make you ruler over many things. Enter into the joy of your lord.'"

I am sure that the one thing we would all want to hear on the return of Our Master is the words: *"'Well done, good and faithful servant; you were faithful over a few things,* I will make you ruler over many things. Enter into the joy of your lord.'" For us to expect those words, we first need to recognize that we are stewards who received varied entrustments in life, and we need to administer those entrustments on behalf of the One who gave them to us, and secondly, who will come back and hold us to account for what we did with what He gave us. Everything we have, we received from God. We are mere blessed people entrusted with someone else's property.

## Stewardship is about rendering to _____ and Caesar

Stewardship is about paying our taxes and honouring God with our income. Jesus taught us to both honor the demand our governments place on us to pay our taxes, but also to honor God with what belongs to Him. *A part of our income belongs to God, and a part of our income belongs to "Caesar."* We pay "Caesar" by way of paying our taxes, and we return to the Lord what is His by returning ten percent of all our income, and by sowing into His Kingdom work.

> Matthew 22:21 (NKJV) "21 They said to Him, "Caesar's."
> And He said to them, "Render therefore to Caesar
> the things that are Caesar's, and to God the things
> that are God's.""

## Tithing

*The first way in which we distinguish ourselves as followers of Jesus is that we return the ownership of all we own over to God.* One of the first steps we take in honouring God for what He entrusted to us is by starting to return to Him what belongs to Him. Ten percent of all we receive belongs to God. Jesus taught on the principle of tithing, and encouraged it.

> Matthew 23:23 (NIV) "[23] "Woe to you, teachers of the
> law and Pharisees, you hypocrites! You give a tenth
> of your spices—mint, dill and cummin. But you
> have neglected the more important matters of the
> law—justice, mercy and faithfulness. You should
> have practiced the latter, without neglecting the
> former.""

### Where does this Principle come from?

It is a Principle that God taught the Israelites through the laws of Moses, even though this was a Principle practiced by Abraham and Jacob long before the Laws of Moses was introduced by God.

> Leviticus 27:30 (NIV) "[30] "A tithe of everything from the
> land, whether grain from the soil or fruit from the

trees, belongs to the Lord; it is holy to
the Lord. [31] Whoever would redeem any of their
tithe must add a fifth of the value to it. [32] Every
tithe of the herd and flock—every tenth animal
that passes under the shepherd's rod—will be holy
to the Lord."

When Jesus taught on the Principle of the Tithe, he knew that
they would claim on their heritage of being children of Abraham and
as such justifying being so meticulous about tithing, so Jesus simply
reminded them to do what Abraham practiced. We as Believers are
also Children of Abraham and we too should take heed to this
teaching of Jesus by doing "the things that Abraham did."

John 8:39 (NIV) "[39] "Abraham is our father," they
answered. "If you were Abraham's children," said
Jesus, "then you would do the things Abraham
did."

### What is a Tithe?

*A "tithe" is ten percent of all your income.* The amount that you
work on to calculate your taxes, is the amount you work on to determine the ten percent that belongs to God.

We learn here that the tithe belongs to the Lord. Earlier we heard
the teaching of Jesus when He said in Matthew 22 verse 21 that we
should "*give to Caesar what belongs to Caesar, and to God what belongs to
God.*" Well, a tenth of all your income belongs to God. By returning
ten percent of all our income to God we ensure the blessings of God
on the remaining 90 percent of our income.

Proverbs 3:9-10 "[9] Honor the Lord with your wealth,
with the firstfruits of all your crops; [10] then your
barns will be filled to overflowing, and your vats
will brim over with new wine."

A. To tithe means to pay a tenth of your income to the Lord. This is figured on your gross amount. If the government uses the gross amount to figure how much they will take, how much more we need to make sure God's amount is figured on that same amount.

B. If you are in business for yourself, you would not figure on the gross amount of sales. You would deduct your expenses first. The balance would be what you would calculate your tithes on.

C. Some would have us to believe that tithes were only for the Jews under the Law of Moses, but we can see that Abraham paid tithes and he practiced this long before the Law existed. Jacob tithed onto the Lord.

Genesis 14:18-20 "[18] Then Melchizedek king of Salem * brought out bread and wine. He was priest of God Most High, [19] and he blessed Abram, saying, "Blessed be Abram by God Most High, Creator * of heaven and earth. [20] And blessed be *[ Or And praise be to] [Or And praise be to] God Most High, who delivered your enemies into your hand." Then Abram gave him a tenth of everything."

Hebrews 7:1-4 "[7:1] This Melchizedek was king of Salem and priest of God Most High. He met Abraham returning from the defeat of the kings and blessed him, [2] and Abraham gave him a tenth of everything. First, his name means "king of righteousness"; then also, "king of Salem" means "king of peace." [3] Without father or mother, without genealogy, without beginning of days or end of life, like the Son of God he remains a priest forever.[4] Just think how great he was: Even the patriarch Abraham gave him a tenth of the plunder!"

Genesis 28:20-22 (NIV) "[20] Then Jacob made a
vow, saying, "If God will be with me and will watch
over me on this journey I am taking and will give
me food to eat and clothes to wear [21] so that I
return safely to my father's household, then
the Lord[f] will be my God[22] and[g] this stone that I
have set up as a pillar will be God's house, and of
all that you give me I will give you a tenth."

D. Israel was instructed by God to pay a tenth part and it was
counted as holy unto the Lord. In Malachi, God considered it robbing
God if one did not pay their tithes.

Leviticus 27:30 "[30] "A tithe of everything from the
land, whether grain from the soil or fruit from the
trees, belongs to the LORD; it is holy to the
LORD."

2 Chronicles 31:5 "[5] As soon as the order went out, the
Israelites generously gave the firstfruits of their
grain, new wine, oil and honey and all that the
fields produced. They brought a great amount, a
tithe of everything."

E. Jesus rebuked the scribes and Pharisees, because they were not
consistent and honest, in upholding *"justice, mercy and faithfulness"*.
One the one hand they religiously applied the law of tithing, and yet
they neglected *'justice, mercy and faithfulness."* He admonished them
to maintain a consistent standard between the diligence with which
they tithed and the way they deal with others. His reference to *"not
neglecting the former"* was a direct reference to tithing.

Matthew 23:23 (NIV) "[23] "Woe to you, teachers of the
law and Pharisees, you hypocrites! You give a tenth
of your spices—mint, dill and cummin. But you

have neglected the more important matters of the law—justice, mercy and faithfulness. You should have practiced the latter, without neglecting the former."

F. We bring our Tithe to the Lord in the Church, or place of Worship, wherever we gather together in His Presence to worship Him along with other Believers.

> Malachi 3:8-11 "[8] "Will a man rob God? Yet you rob me. "But you ask, 'How do we rob you?' "In tithes and offerings. [9] You are under a curse—the whole nation of you—because you are robbing me. [10] Bring the whole tithe into the storehouse, that there may be food in my house. Test me in this," says the LORD Almighty, "and see if I will not throw open the floodgates of heaven and pour out so much blessing that you will not have room enough for it. [11] I will prevent pests from devouring your crops, and the vines in your fields will not cast their fruit," says the LORD Almighty."

Some people think that they can divide their tithe and give a little here, and a little there, but in this instance, the Word of God teaches explicitly to *bring the whole tithe into the storehouse*". The storehouse is directly linked to *my house*," meaning the Place of Worship. As Believers we embrace God's Word as a guideline for living in the blessing of God. Tithing is just one way in which we can become good stewards of God's resources.

> Malachi 3:8 "[8] "Will a man rob God? Yet you rob me. "But you ask, 'How do we rob you?' "In tithes and offerings."

~

Philippians 4:19 "[19] And my God will meet all your
needs according to his glorious riches in Christ
Jesus."

G. We are to pay our tithes first, before we pay anyone else. If we
pay God first, He will help us take care of the rest of our bills. But if
we wait until we can afford to pay our tithes, we will not have enough
money to pay them. That is why God says to prove Him, because it
will not work out on paper.

God's mathematics is far above ours. He can stretch our finances
when we dedicate them to Him. Not only will he help us pay our
bills, He will pour out a blessing on us that there will not be enough
room for us to receive it.

### Offerings

Tithing is returning to God what belongs to Him, however, then
only does our giving starts. Our generosity starts when we start
taking what belongs to us, and start investing it into the work of God.
People spend their money and resources on all kind of things,
however, for us as Believers, it should be a reflection of our heart for
God. One of the ways in which we display this is by our possessions,
the things we have and what we do with our possessions.

### Possessions

One of the things Jesus taught His Disciples was to be careful and
moderate on the intent they place on the accumulation on possessions. We are good stewards when we choose to rather store up for
ourselves treasures in Heaven than on earth.

Matthew 6:20-21 "[20] But store up for yourselves
treasures in heaven, where moth and rust do not
destroy, and where thieves do not break in and

steal. [21] For where your treasure is, there your heart will be also."

May the balance with which we spend our income and resources truly reflect our devotion and love for God and His work. The early church quickly became known for their yieldedness to God and His work by their generosity towards the Church and His Work.

> Acts 2:44-45 (NIV) "[44] All the believers were together and had everything in common. [45] They sold property and possessions to give to anyone who had need."

> Acts 4:32-35 (NIV) "[32] All the believers were one in heart and mind. No one claimed that any of their possessions was their own, but they shared everything they had. [33] With great power the apostles continued to testify to the resurrection of the Lord Jesus. And God's grace was so powerfully at work in them all [34] that there were no needy persons among them. For from time to time those who owned land or houses sold them, brought the money from the sales [35] and put it at the apostles' feet, and it was distributed to anyone who had need."

By honouring God, or sowing into God's work, we unlock the "harvest" potential through the seed we sow. The Harvest is always disproportionate against the seed that was sown. The reward for honouring God and His work is also disproportionate.

Paying our tithes and offerings keeps our heart into the kingdom of God. We are investing in our future and the future of our children. It takes money to operate any business, and God's work is no exception. He can do it without our money, but when we give, we share in the victory and blessing that God wants to pour out on His people. Give with the right attitude. It is a form of worship.

## Good Stewardship

God wants us to be good stewards over His resources, so, here are a couple of things we need to know from God's Word.

### A. Pay your taxes.

God wants us to pay our taxes as good citizens of the countries where He placed us.

> Matthew 22:21 (NKJV) "21 They said to Him, "Caesar's."
> And He said to them, "Render therefore to Caesar
> the things that are Caesar's, and to God the things
> that are God's."

We might not be living in Roman times, but we sure live in countries where it is required that we pay taxes. We honor God when we pay our taxes.

### B. Don't sign surety for anyone.

> Proverbs 6:1-5 "[6:1] My son, if you have put up security
> for your neighbor, if you have struck hands in
> pledge for another, [2] if you have been trapped by
> what you said, ensnared by the words of your
> mouth, [3] then do this, my son, to free yourself,
> since you have fallen into your neighbour's hands:
> Go and humble yourself; press your plea with your
> neighbor! [4] Allow no sleep to your eyes, no
> slumber to your eyelids. [5] Free yourself, like a
> gazelle from the hand of the hunter, like a bird

from the snare of the fowler. [6] Go to the ant, you
sluggard; consider its ways and be wise!"

Proverbs 11:15 "[15] He who puts up security for another
will surely suffer, but whoever refuses to strike
hands in pledge is safe."

## C. Get out of debt.

As a new believer, your finances might be in shambles. God wants us
to get out of debt, but this can take some time. We didn't get into our
mess overnight, and it will take time to straighten out, but it can be
straightened out with obedience to God's word and diligence.

Proverbs 22:1, 7 "[22:1] A good name is more desirable
than great riches; to be esteemed is better than
silver or gold. [7] The rich rule over the poor, and
the borrower is servant to the lender."
Romans 13:8 "[8] Let no debt remain outstanding,
except the continuing debt to love one another, for
he who loves his fellowman has fulfilled the law."

## D. Contentment

1 Timothy 6:6 "But godliness with contentment is great
gain."

To be content is a huge value in the Kingdom of God, and there
for one of the essential values in the spiritual discipline of Stewardship.

~

### Afterword

God wants to bless us so we can bless others. If we are poor managers of our finances, we will never be able to help others. There is a wealth of knowledge in the Bible concerning money management. We need to be responsible for paying our bills, having a good name, and not being lazy. Don't live beyond your means, or spending more than what you earn. Learn to be content and wait until you can afford things to buy them.

### God desires to bless your finances

God has a plan, a blessed plan, for each of us. One of the ways in which He wants to bless us is in our finances.

> Jeremiah 29:11 (NIV) "11. For I know the plans I have for you," declares the Lord, "plans to prosper you and not to harm you, plans to give you hope and a future."

# PART II

---

# VALUES OF THE KINGDOM
# OF GOD

# 2

# CONSERVATIVE

**Definition:**

*To be conservative is the considered choice of living rather carefully than liberally.* It is the making of careful and conservative choices within the guidelines of the Bible. You would rather err on being too conservative than allowing yourself liberties that might be frowned upon by God.

**Scriptures:**

> Matthew 7:13-14 (NIV) "13 "Enter through the narrow gate. For wide is the gate and broad is the road that leads to destruction, and many enter through it. 14 But small is the gate and narrow the road that leads to life, and only a few find it."

> Matthew 5:28-29 (NIV), 1 Corinthians 10:23-24, 31-33 (NIV), Colossians 3:17 (NIV)

**Characteristic explained:**

The Bible is a Handbook on conservative and considered living. When we consider the many laws and commandments God gave His people, we observe that they are rules and guidelines for conservative and considered living. Firstly, we apply the Word of God to our actions and reactions, and then we consider the way it might impact others, and then we also consider how others might view our behaviour, but most of all, how would God view my behaviour.

**Life Application:**

The Scriptures we explored on Conservative living, to name a few, direct our attention to make decisions, more on the conservative side, than on the liberal side of life. Scripture clearly teaches us to be considered in our liberties, especially as it might negatively affect or impact a weaker person in their faith. I pray that God will help us value being "Conservative" more than being seen as liberal, broad-minded and "with it." It is a Value in the Kingdom of God to be intentionally more conservative than liberal.

## 3

# FRUIT-BEARING

**Definition:**

To be fruit bearing is to both exhibit the change Christ brought into one's own life as well as bearing fruit through successfully leading others to follow Christ as well. Fruit-bearing is neither the one nor the other, it is both simultaneous, consistent and enduring.

**Scriptures:**

> Matthew 7:16-18 (NIV) 16 By their fruit you will recognize them. Do people pick grapes from thorn bushes, or figs from thistles? 17 Likewise every good tree bears good fruit, but a bad tree bears bad fruit. 18 A good tree cannot bear bad fruit, and a bad tree cannot bear good fruit.

> Matthew 12:33 (NIV), Matthew 13:23 (NIV), Matthew 21:43 (NIV)

**Characteristic explained:**

One of the most powerful ways in which we show and proof our legitimacy as Children of God, who turned from our wicked ways unto the living God, is to bear the fruit of a changed life in our lives. It is also the ability to reproduce after our own, renewed, self. We can tell people all we want, but what they really hear and learn is what we model with our lives.

**Life Application:**

The best way to apply this Kingdom Value is by daily considering the miracle of salvation, and being born again. When we consider the work of God in us, we can't but be filled with a deep appreciation of His wondrous recreative and renewal work. This daily reminder should inspire us to live close to the renewed Nature of God in us. When we are born again, we become one in spirit with God. We are born of the Holy Spirit. It is the nature of the Holy Spirit in us that should be lived and seen by everyone around us. If He directs and reigns supremely, then He will bring forth everlasting fruit in us. Make it your life ambition to be a bearer of Good fruit.

# 4

## PRACTITIONER

**Definition:**

*Practitioners show that they value the Kingdom of God by being doers of the Word.* Jesus values doers, those putting things He teaches into practice in their lives.

**Scriptures:**

> Matthew 7:24 (NIV) The Wise and Foolish Builders "24 "Therefore everyone who hears these words of mine and puts them into practice is like a wise man who built his house on the rock."

> John 14:23 (NIV), James 1:22 (NIV), Romans 2:13 (NIV), Luke 6:47-49 (NIV), Luke 8:21 (NIV), Philippians 4:9 (NIV)

**Characteristic explained:**

The way Jesus taught us, we can't but apply this value to our lives. Who doesn't want to be seen as a wise man? Who of us want to be seen to be a fool? None of us want to be seen to be foolish. This value places a high premium on doing and applying the teachings of Jesus, against simply just hearing it, talking about it or telling others to do it.

**Life Application:**

*We value being a practitioner when we daily consider how we may put the Word of God*, from our morning devotions, *into practice in our lives*. God loves doers. The Lord delights in those who put His words into practice. Take time every morning to consider how you will put His Teachings into practice.

Think of ways in which you can apply His teachings to the way you speak, the things you do or actions you could take in certain situations in which you could and should take action. We show our love to Christ when we do whatever He asks of us. Obedience is seen in how we put the teachings of Jesus into practice.

# 5

## ACCOUNTABILITY

**Definition:**

*Accountability is to value living answerable for one's actions, deeds and words*, both to man and God. Accountability is expressed by taking responsibility for one's actions and words.

**Scriptures:**

> Matthew 12:36 (NIV) 12 "But I tell you that men will
> have to give account on the day of judgement for
> every careless word they have spoken."

> Romans 14:12 (NIV) "12 So then, each of us will give an
> account of ourselves to God."

> Hebrews 4:13 (NIV), 1 Peter 4:5 (NIV), Colossians
> 4:6 (NIV)

## Characteristic explained:

Accountability is one of the essential qualities of a mature person. *Accountability is to take responsibility for one's actions.* Being accountable means that one is answerable, takes responsibility and liable.

## Life Application:

*God desires that we live answerable for whatever we do.* Making decisions based on the fact that you take liability for what you say and do shows that you have become accountable. It is easy to pass the buck or shift the blame when things go wrong, however, it is a Value in the Kingdom of God to take responsibility and assume liability when it is needed. Many people live a life in denial or blaming others for everything that happens in their lives. They blame others for their actions, behaviour and the way they respond, but God desires that we live answerable for our own actions, not just to others, but also as it relates to God.

## 6

---

# LIVING BY FAITH

**Definition:**

Faith believes beyond proof. Faith is doing things because of what you belief to be true. Faith is acting purely because God said you should or could. Our actions flow from what we truly belief.

**Scriptures:**

> Matthew 17:20 (NIV) 20 He replied, "Because you have so little faith. I tell you the truth, if you have faith as small as a mustard seed, you can say to this mountain, 'Move from here to there' and it will move. Nothing will be impossible for you.'"

> Romans 1:17 (NIV) 17 For in the gospel a righteousness from God is revealed, a righteousness that is by faith from first to last, just as it is written: "The righteous will live by faith."

Hebrews 11:1 (NIV) Faith in Action "1 Now faith is confidence in what we hope for and assurance about what we do not see."

## Characteristic explained:

*Having Faith is that ability to live with hope, assurance and trust that the future is good and that everything will work out.* Having faith is that confident reliance in someone or something. Faith is to have strong conviction in what you belief. Faith is expressed and seen by our loyalty, commitment and devotion.

## Life Application:

As Believers, we give expression to the strong faith and believe we have in the Triune God, that we undergird every situation with hope and assurance that God is in control and that His Will, will be done. As Believers we give expression to our faith by our loyal commitment and devotion to the teachings of Christ. Believers are loyal people. We are people whom people can trust and rely on. We are positive and express our assurance in the Almighty God's Sovereignty in everything that we might face and go through. *We are always hopeful, faithful, reliant, committed, and loyal.*

# 7

# CHILDLIKENESS

**Definition:**

*Childlikeness is the heart attitude of humility towards God, expressed by simple obedience in action.* Those who value childlikeness take the Words of the Lord Jesus literally and apply it without trying to dissect or interpret it. They simply do what is asked.

**Scriptures:**

> Matthew 18:3-5 (NIV) 3 And he said: "I tell you the truth, unless you change and become like little children, you will never enter the kingdom of heaven. 4 Therefore, whoever humbles himself like this child is the greatest in the kingdom of heaven. 5 And whoever welcomes a little child like this in my name welcomes me."

**Characteristic explained:**

*This value is characterised by simple faith, obedience and childlikeness.*
Jesus explained this value by defining what it requires. He defined
that it requires humility to enter the Kingdom of God. Jesus came to
teach us about the Kingdom of Heaven. Whenever you hear the word
"Kingdom," you have a King and His Kingdom. No democratically
determined, popularised ideas are welcomed in the Kingdom of God.
It takes simple faith and trust to belief that whatever Jesus taught was
well considered and has as a predetermined outcome, our best
interest at heart. Childlikeness determines to trust the Lord's judg-
ment and determination as final and conclusive.

**Life Application:**

We act and value childlikeness when we apply simple faith and trust
to put the words of Jesus into practice in our lives. It never ceases to
amaze me how strong certain cultures are around the world, simply
for applying childlike faith to their daily living. The greatest advancement of the Gospel appears among those who are still moved by the
simple instructions of the Lord. They act and do without questioning
or doubting the Lord's guidance and instruction.

> Mark 16:18 (NIV) "18 they will pick up snakes with their
> hands; and when they drink deadly poison, it will
> not hurt them at all; they will place their hands-on
> sick people, and they will get well."

Childlike faith is what I grew up on. My Dad quoted Mark 16:18
every time he prayed for us when we were unwell. We had childlike
faith to believe that what the Bible said was true and we embraced
our healing since Dad acted on the Word of God. Let us be those who
add this value of the Kingdom of God to our lives.

# 8

# UNITY

**Definition:**

Unity is expressed by a heart attitude that desires to work together with others and seek to find mutual agreement and cooperation for the sake of Christ.

**Scriptures:**

> Matthew 18:19 (NIV) "19 "Again, I tell you that if two of
> you on earth agree about anything you ask for, it
> will be done for you by my Father in heaven."

> John 21:20-23 (NIV), Acts 4:32 (NIV), 1 Corinthians 1:10
> (NIV), Psalms 133:1 and 3 (NIV), Amos 3:3 (NIV)

**Characteristic explained:**

One another statements are frequent throughout the New Testament. God desires His children to live at peace and in agreement with one another. The Lord desires that we are ONE. The Lord desires that through us living in unity and agreement with one another, that people will belief and put their faith in God. Unity, cooperation and agreement lies at the heart of those who belong to the Kingdom of God. It stems from our own humility to advance the purposes and desires of our King. The very heart of our relationship with the Triune God is set in agreement through the covenant relationship we entered into through the Blood of Jesus. Unity is defined for us by our covenant relationship with God, Every time we partake of the Table of the Lord, we affirm our agreement, our covenant relationship with God.

**Life Application:**

*We are the Body of Christ and Unity is vitally important to our health and sustenance.* As an expression of our covenant relationship with God through the shed Blood of Jesus, we always work towards the best interest of our mutually bound covenant partners. We live in an era where individualism is prized, however, in the Kingdom of God we prize and value agreement and unity. It is such a stark value to observe when people put away their own wants and preferences to work towards that that builds collaboration and unity.

Unity is what God desires. As Children of God we show our Kingdom Values when we openly put away our own preferences in favor of that which will bring agreement and unity. Take steps every day to work together with others. Harness yourself to set aside your wants and desires and to be willing to build unity wherever you work. The level of unity determines the level of impact we have in this world. God commands His blessing where there is unity and agreement.

# PART III

# ASSIMILATION SHEET

### Spiritual Discipline: Stewardship

1.  Complete the sentence. *"Good stewardship requires* _____.*"*

2. Complete the sentence. *"Stewardship is about being* _____ *to God."*_____

3. Stewardship is about rendering to Caesar what is his and to God what is His. What does this mean to you? _____
_____
_____

4. What is a Tithe? _____

5. Name four things that define us as good stewards of the resources God gave us?

_____

_____

## Values of the Kingdom of God

6. What does it means to value being *"Conservative"*? _____

_____

_____

_____

7. *"Fruit-bearing"* is a Kingdom Value. Why are we expected to bear fruit? _____

_____

_____

8. What Scripture speaks to you most about being a *"Practitioner"*?

_____

_____

_____

_____

9. How can you be more *"Accountable"*?

_____

_____

_____

_____

10. What does it mean to be *"Living by Faith"*?

_____

_____

_____

_____

_____

# WEEK SIX

# PART I

## SPIRITUAL DISCIPLINE - WORSHIP

# 1

## WORSHIP

Jesus taught His Disciples *the spiritual discipline of worship.* The first part of the "*Lord's Prayer*" is devoted to "*Hallowing Our Father in Heaven.*" In the Gospel of John He teaches us that the Father is "*looking for worshippers.*" Worship was never, and should never be confined to what we do during our time of Worship during our weekly church services. Worship is sometime we do daily, and we intentionally dedicate time to worship God privately and corporately.

> "*Worship is the Spiritual Discipline of spending dedicated time to fellowship with the Father, His Son and the Holy Spirit, in loving, worshipping and adoring Him with all your heart, mind, soul and strength.*"

Jesus taught us that worship is important. God dwells in the praises of His people. The First commandment is to "*love the Lord your God with all your heart, with all your soul, with all your mind, and with all your strength.*" What better way is there to take time to worship Him on a daily basis and to give expression of your love for the Lord.

John 4:23-24 (NKJV) 23 But the hour is coming, and
now is, when the true worshipers will worship the
Father in spirit and truth; for the Father is seeking
such to worship Him. 24 God is Spirit, and those
who worship Him must worship in spirit and truth.

Mark 12:29-30 (NKJV) 29 Jesus answered him, "The first
of all the commandments is: 'Hear, O Israel, the
Lord our God, the Lord is one. 30 And you shall
love the Lord your God with all your heart, with all
your soul, with all your mind, and with all your
strength.' This is the first commandment.

Isaiah 40:31 (NKJV) "31 But those who wait on the Lord
shall renew their strength; They shall mount up
with wings like eagles. They shall run and not be
weary, They shall walk and not faint."

**Prayer is practised by all Faiths**

One of the most profound spiritual disciplines practiced by all
faiths is that of taking time to "worship" and pray daily. Whenever
you enter the house of a Hindu you see their altar where they
worship their gods and offer their prayers. Whenever you enter the
house of a Buddhist or Muslim you will find a dedicated place of
prayer and worship.

As Believers, we too take time to have fellowship with the Father,
the Son and the Holy Spirit. The early Church practiced the discipline of fellowship and worship daily.

1 John 1:3 (NIV) "3 We proclaim to you what we have
seen and heard, so that you also may have
fellowship with us. And our fellowship is with the
Father and with His Son, Jesus Christ."

Acts 2:42 (NIV) "42 They devoted themselves to the
Apostles' teaching and to fellowship, to the
breaking of bread and to _____."

The spiritual discipline of "WORSHIP" is practiced when we daily take time to worship God and have fellowship with the Triune God.

*Worship is the act of "self-surrender" as well as "a time of adoring" the Almighty God.*

### Defining the meaning of Worship

Worshipping the Lord, in a simple sense, might best be described as "*a silent surrender of the soul to God, and the adoration of God*". Many great men and woman of prayer through the years have shared so much wisdom on Worship and Prayer.

*F W Robertson said:*
*"Life is most holy in which there is least of petition and desire, and more of waiting upon God; that in which petition most often passes into thanksgiving. Pray till prayer makes you forget your own wishes and leave it or merge it into God's will."*

## Worship is a time during which we surrender _____ before God.

I think that the greatest worship we can bring God is to bring ourselves in full surrender to Him. Surrendering to Him through worship and adoration gives expression of our worship of Him. Through submission we humble ourselves, and that is one of the greatest expressions of Worship of God.

James 4:7 (NIV) "7 _____ yourselves, then,
to God. Resist the devil, and he will flee from you.

James 4:10 (NIV) "[10] _____ yourselves before the Lord, and he will lift you up."

*David McIntyre wrote a century ago;*
*"When prayer rises to its truest level, self, with its concerns and needs*
*forgotten to time and the interests of Christ fill, and sometimes overwhelm,*
*the soul. It is then that prayer becomes most urgent and intense."*

Worship is not just praise or thanksgiving, although it is very closely related and normally naturally flows directly from it. In fact, often our time of praise overlap into worship.

### We worship best when we are _____

I've sensed through the years that out of a grateful heart (thanksgiving), the praise of God follows and result into a time of deep worship and adoration of God. Praise might best be described as a vocal focus on the nature and love of God and *worship **a silent focus on being close and intimate with Him.***

Worship takes time. It takes time to enter into deep worship. We should therefor set aside sufficient time in our daily schedule to *"wait on the Lord"*, *"to renew our strength"*, and to simply worship and adore Him. Sometimes WORSHIP results from my time of WAITING and other times my time of WAITING results into a deep and meaningful time of deep WORSHIP.

### Worship takes, and requires _____

A good relationship is the result of dedicating time to the relationship. TIME is the factor in Worship and being in Fellowship with God. When time has been moved out of the equation for you to spend time with the Living God, it would bring such a transformation in your life that you would have more time and accomplish more in the time available. I have found that entering into that place and space of worship come more frequent and quicker, as years go by, than when I started pursuing the Presence of God in my earlier years of walking with God.

## Silent Focus

Perhaps an example from marital life would help illustrate this point. Each day, and quite often, I say to my wife; "*I love you.*" This is an expression of my love and adoration in words.

Then, there are times when I take her into my arms and I simply hold her near me. This is a silent moment of adoration. True, I may use these moments to verbalise my love with statements like, "*I love you,*" or "*I appreciate you.*" However, the real focus in these moments is simply that of being together.

Similarly, prayer needs these times of quiet sharing. Without this spiritual intimacy with God prayer would be shallow.

## Supernatural focus

True Worship then should begin not with asking but with a focus on relationship. Asking must come later. True friendship means sharing: shared resources, shared lives, shared time. Such must be our desire with God in prayer and worship. We must seek, merely to be with Him.

> *Andrew Murray wrote:*
> *"He who in prayer has no time in quietness of soul, and in full consciousness of its meaning to say Abba, Father, has missed the best part of prayer."*

To a large degree our time of waiting on God might be termed "*wordless worship*". It is a spiritual love affair, a supernatural union.

Prayer is something deeper than words. It is present in the soul long before it has been formulated in words. And it abides in the soul long after the last words of prayer have passed over our lips.

## Worship prepares us for a meaningful time of Prayer

Worship and waiting in the Presence of God prepares us for all that will follow in a meaningful time of prayer.

*"The dew falls most copiously when the night winds are hushed."*

## Worship is a time to adore

I pray that you will 1. Dedicate a place, like your bedroom or office or veranda, where you will take time to pray and to worship God. This is the place where you will have fellowship with God; and 2. Set aside a dedicated time to pray, but more than it being a time of asking or petitioning, that it be a time of adoration and worship of God with all your heart, soul, mind and strength.

> Luke 11:2-3 (NKJV) "2 So He said to them, "When you pray, say: "Our Father in heaven, Hallowed be Your name. May Your Kingdom come. Your will be done on earth as it is in heaven. 3 Give us today our daily bread. "

## Worship precedes deep and meaningful prayer

For an enduring encounter with Almighty God we need to set aside time at the beginning of our daily time with God to Worship Him. Worship is a time to adore our Heavenly Father for who He is and what He means to us. One very helpful way is to take use the Names of God alongside which we express our adoration.

> Isaiah 9:6 (NIV) "⁶ For to us a child is born, to us a son is given, and the government will be on his shoulders. And he will be called Wonderful Counselor, Mighty God, Everlasting Father, Prince of Peace."

## JEHOVAH SHALOM

Jehovah Shalom, He is our _____, He gives us Rest. He brings us to a place of Contentment.

> Isaiah 53:5 [5] But he was pierced for our
> transgressions, he was crushed for our iniquities;
> the punishment that brought us peace was upon
> him, and by his wounds we are healed.

> Hebrews 4:9-10 [9] There remains, then, a Sabbath-rest
> for the people of God; [10] for anyone who enters
> God's rest also rests from his own work, just as God
> did from his.

> John 14:27 [27] Peace I leave with you; my peace I give
> you. I do not give to you as the world gives. Do not
> let your hearts be troubled and do not be afraid.

## JEHOVAH TZIDKENU

Jehovah Tzidkenu, He is our Righteousness. He forgives us of all our sins.

> 2 Corinthians 5:21 [21] God made him who had no sin
> to be sin for us, so that in him we might become
> the righteousness of God.

> 1 Corinthians 1:30 [30] It is because of him that you are
> in Christ Jesus, who has become for us wisdom
> from God—that is, our righteousness, holiness and
> redemption.

> Romans 1:17 [17] For in the gospel a righteousness from
> God is revealed, a righteousness that is by faith

from first to last, just as it is written: "The righteous
will live by faith."

## JEHOVAH M'KADDESH

Jehovah M'Kaddesh, He is the One who _____ and Purifies
us.

> 1 Corinthians 6:9-11 [9] Do you not know that the
> wicked will not inherit the kingdom of God? Do
> not be deceived: Neither the sexually immoral nor
> idolaters nor adulterers nor male prostitutes nor
> homosexual offenders [10] nor thieves nor the
> greedy nor drunkards nor slanderers nor swindlers
> will inherit the kingdom of God. [11] And that is
> what some of you were. But you were washed, you
> were sanctified, you were justified in the name of
> the Lord Jesus Christ and by the Spirit of our God.

> 1 Thessalonians 5:23 [23] May God himself, the God of
> peace, sanctify you through and through. May your
> whole spirit, soul and body be kept blameless at
> the coming of our Lord Jesus Christ.

## JEHOVAH SHAMMAH

Jehovah Shammah, The LORD Is THERE. He is _____.
He is with us always.

> Ezekiel 48:35b "And the name of the city from that time
> on will be: **THE LORD IS THERE.**"

> Ephesians 2:21-22 [21] In him the whole building is
> joined together and rises to become a holy temple
> in the Lord. [22] And in him you too are being built

together to become **a dwelling in which God lives by his Spirit.**

Hebrews 13:5

[5] Keep your lives free from the love of money and be content with what you have, because God has said, **"Never will I leave you; never will I forsake you."**

Deuteronomy 31:6

[6] Be strong and courageous. Do not be afraid or terrified because of them, for **the LORD your God goes with you; he will never leave you nor forsake you."**

## JEHOVAH RAPHA

Jehovah Rapha, He is the Lord our _____. He heals us of all our diseases.

Exodus 15:26

[26] And said, If thou wilt diligently hearken to the voice of the LORD thy God, and wilt do that which is right in his sight, and wilt give ear to his commandments, and keep all his statutes, I will put none of these diseases upon thee, which I have brought upon the Egyptians: for I am the LORD that healeth thee."

Exodus 23:25-26

"[25] Worship the LORD your God, and his blessing will be on your food and water. I will take away sickness from among you, [26] and none will miscarry or be barren in your land. I will give you a full life span."

1 Peter 2:24 "[24] He himself bore our sins in his body on the tree, so that we might die to sins and live for righteousness; by his wounds you have been healed."

Psalm 147:3 "[3] He heals the broken-hearted and binds up their wounds."

## JEHOVAH JIREH

Jehovah Jireh, He is the One Who Sees and _____ for us.

Genesis 22:14 [14] So Abraham called that place The LORD Will Provide. And to this day it is said, "On the mountain of the LORD it will be provided."

Psalm 34:15-18 "[15] The eyes of the LORD are on the righteous and his ears are attentive to their cry; [16] the face of the LORD is against those who do evil, to cut off the memory of them from the earth. [17] The righteous cry out, and the LORD hears them; he delivers them from all their troubles. [18] The LORD is close to the brokenhearted and saves those who are crushed in spirit. [19] A righteous man may have many troubles, but the LORD delivers him from them all;"

## JEHOVAH NISSI

Jehovah Nissi, the Lord is our Banner, and the Captain of the Host. He gives us the victory over our enemies.

Genesis 17:15-16 [15] Moses built an altar and called it **The LORD is my Banner.** [16] He said, "For hands were lifted up to the throne of the LORD. The

LORD will be at war against the Amalekites from
generation to generation."

Isaiah 11:10 [10] In that day the Root of Jesse will stand
as **a banner for the peoples**; the nations will rally
to him, and his place of rest will be glorious.

2 Corinthians 2:14 [14] But thanks be to God, **who
always leads us in triumphal procession in Christ**
and through us spreads everywhere the fragrance
of the knowledge of him.

## JEHOVAH ROHI

Jehovah Rohi, the Lord is my _____. He is my constant
Companion and Friend.

Hebrews 11:6 [6] But without faith it is impossible to
please him: for he that cometh to God must believe
that he is, and that **he is a rewarder of them that
diligently seek him.**

Psalm 23:1-3 [1] **The LORD is my shepherd**; I shall not
be in want. [2] He makes me lie down in green
pastures, he leads me beside quiet waters, [3] he
restores my soul. He guides me in paths of
righteousness for his name's sake."

1Peter 2:25" For you were like sheep going astray, but
now you have returned to **the Shepherd and
Overseer of your souls."**

**YESHUA**

Jesus is our Saviour!

> Exodus 15:2 [2] The LORD is my strength and my song; **he has become my salvation.** He is my God, and I will praise him, my father's God, and I will exalt him. [3] The LORD is a warrior; the LORD is his name.

> Isaiah 12:2-3 [2] Surely **God is my salvation;** I will trust and not be afraid. The LORD, the LORD, is my strength and my song; **he has become my salvation.** [3] With joy you will draw water from the wells of salvation.

> Matthew 1:21 [21] She will give birth to a son, and you are to give him the name **Jesus,** because **he will save his people from their sins.**

> Acts 4:12 [12] **Salvation is found in no one else,** for there is no other name under heaven given to men by which we must be saved.

Worship is that time at the beginning, and often in conclusion of our time with God, where we express our heartfelt adoration to Him for who He is and what He means to us. Worship is also our way of saying that we place our entire trust in Him as the Source and Hope of our lives.

# PART II

## VALUES OF THE KINGDOM OF GOD

# 2

---

# SERVANTHOOD

**Definition:**

Servanthood is the value of serving and helping others for their benefit and good.

**Scriptures:**

> Matthew 20:26-28 (NIV) "26 Not so with you. Instead, **whoever wants to become great among you must be your servant,** 27 and **whoever wants to be first must be your slave**– 28 just as the **Son of Man did not come to be served, but to serve,** and to give his life as a ransom for many."

> Ephesians 6:7-8 (NIV), Colossians 3:23-24 (NIV), Romans 12:11 (NIV), 1 Peter 4:10 (NIV), Galatians 5:13 (NIV)

**Characteristic explained:**

*Servanthood is the internal value of helping others.* Being a servant requires humility, and an ability to give yourself to the benefit of others. Servanthood is at the top of the values defining Great Leaders in the Kingdom of God. Great Leaders in the Kingdom of God are characterised by their serving.

**Life Application:**

We value Servanthood when we go out of our way to help others. It is the selfless act of stepping into a situation to assist others with something they need help with. We need to do so wholeheartedly, with love, diligently, not just please men but to please God. Seek opportunities each day to serve others.

# 3

---

# LOYALTY

**Definition:**

To be Loyal is to be committed. Loyalty is the allegiance one commits to.

**Scriptures:**

> Luke 9:62 (KJV) "[62] And Jesus said unto him, **No man, having put his hand to the plough, and looking back, is fit for the kingdom of God.**"

> Psalm 37:5, John 15:13

**Characteristic explained:**

Children of God, Believers, are characterised by their commitment and loyalty to the Kingdom of God. They start and finish tasks. They don't give up when things are tough or hard. They stick to the task and assignment before them. Loyalty is shown by the extent to which one is prepared to stay committed to someone. People who are loyal are dependable, faithful and trustworthy. They are defined by their reliability and steadfastness. Loyal people are constantly steadfast in their dedication.

**Life Application:**

We all love to have loyal people around us. The best gift we could be to others is to be constantly steadfast in our dedication in our work. We truly value loyalty when we show dependable commitment to stick to a plan even when it proves to be tough to conclude or succeed. Make a commitment to be someone whom people can depend on, who are faithful and trustworthy. Loyalty is a characteristic of those who truly follow their Lord steadfastly.

The question we need to ask ourselves sometimes is:

- *How reliable am I?*
- *How trustworthy am I?*
- *How steadfast and dependable am I?*

Make a decision to be that loyal, reliable and trustworthy friend people can turn to. Be that dependable, faithful and steadfast person.

# 4

## GRATEFULNESS

**Definition:**

Gratitude is the feeling you have, or express, of appreciation for something you have, or received, or observed.

**Scriptures:**

> 1 Thessalonians 5:18 "In everything give thanks: for this
> is the will of God in Christ Jesus concerning you."

> Colossians 3:16 (NIV) "16 Let the message of Christ
> dwell among you richly as you teach and
> admonish one another with all wisdom through
> psalms, hymns, and songs from the Spirit, singing
> to God with gratitude in your hearts."

> Psalms 100:4-5 (NIV) 4 Enter his gates with
> thanksgiving and his courts with praise; give
> thanks to him and praise his name. 5 For the Lord

is good and his love endures forever; his
faithfulness continues through all generations.

## Characteristic explained:

Gratitude is the expression of appreciation and thanks for some
blessing one observed in one's life. Gratitude is being thankful,
appreciative and grateful. The Psalmist teaches us to enter His Gates
with Thanksgiving in our hearts.

## Life Application:

We value gratitude when we take time every day and firstly observe
the many things, we could be grateful for, and secondly, express
appreciation to those who made it possible.

A question to ask is:

- Am I a grateful person?
- How often do I give expression of my gratitude to others
  and to God, acknowledging them, and Him, for the
  blessings we observe?

Take time and count your blessings, and if possible, give expression to those to whom you are able to express yourself for those blessings. Believers are grateful people. Believers say *"Thank you."* Believers express appreciation and gratitude. Give thanks!

5
---

# STEWARDSHIP

**Definition:**

Stewardship is proofing oneself faithful as a steward with the Gifts, talents and resources of the King. Stewardship is embracing the accountability, and faithfully administering the resources as directed by the Lord.

**Scriptures:**

> Matthew 17:24-27 (NIV) [24] After Jesus and his
>     disciples arrived in Capernaum, the collectors of
>     the two-drachma tax came to Peter and asked,
>     "Doesn't your teacher pay the temple tax?"
>     [25] "Yes, he does," he replied. When Peter came
>     into the house, Jesus was the first to speak. "What
>     do you think, Simon?" he asked. "From whom do
>     the kings of the earth collect duty and taxes—from
>     their own sons or from others?" [26] "From others,"
>     Peter answered. "Then the sons are exempt," Jesus

said to him. [27] "But so that we may not offend them, go to the lake and throw out your line. Take the first fish you catch; open its mouth and you will find a four-drachma coin. Take it and give it to them for my tax and yours."

Matthew 22:21 (NIV) [21] "Caesar's," they replied. Then he said to them, "Give to Caesar what is Caesar's, and to God what is God's."

Matthew 25:21 (NIV), 1 Peter 4:10 (NIV), Matthew 22:17-21 (NIV)

## Characteristic explained:

We value good stewardship when we pay our taxes and honour God with the First fruit of all our income. Stewardship is defined by being a person who has been entrusted with something special, and of worth, and administers the entrustment with faithfulness and care. Stewardship speaks of trustworthiness, reliability and care. Stewardship speaks of noble character.

## Life Application:

We are good stewards if we faithfully administer the things God entrusted to us. Joseph was such a faithful steward over the Household of Potiphar.

God later rewarded Joseph's faithful Stewardship by entrusting to him the resources of an entire nation. We all have a dream of being welcomed into our eternal home with the words: *"Welcome Home, Good and Faithful Servant."* For us to receive such a welcome we need to see ourselves as stewards, being entrusted with the assets of our Lord. We are not really owners; we are stewards of the entrustments to us. May we be able to show how diligently we administered the gifts, talents and resources he entrusted to us.

A good question to ask, firstly is:

- *What are the things that I believe God entrusted to me?*
- *Am I a good steward of it?*
- *Am I administering it as unto Him and for the advancement of His Kingdom?*

I pray that God will find in each one of us a Faithful and Good Steward.

# 6

# OBEDIENCE

**Definition:**

Obedience is expressed by the way we fully comply and execute that which is expected, asked and demanded of us.

**Scriptures:**

> Luke 11:28 (NIV) "28 He replied, "Blessed rather are those who hear the word of God and obey it.""

> John 8:55 (NIV) "55 Though you do not know him, I know him. If I said I did not, I would be a liar like you, but I do know him and obey his word.""

> John 14:23-24 (NIV), Acts 5:29 (NIV), Acts 5:32 (NIV), Romans 6:17 (NIV), Matthew 28:20 (NIV), Ephesians 6:1 (NIV), 2 John 1:6 (NIV), Hebrews 5:8-9 (NIV), Deuteronomy 28:1-13 describes the blessings of obedience to God.

**Characteristic explained:**

Obedience is the value of submissive and decisive adherence. Obedience is to respect God by complying and living in agreement with what he said and want. Obedience is the ability to yield and to conform to the Will of Him who Called, instructed and directed you to do something. The Blessings of Abraham are reserved for those who walk in obedience to His Will and Purpose.

**Life Application:**

There is tremendous Power in obedience and submitting to the Will of God. Naaman got healed when he obeyed and went to dip himself in the Jordan River. The widow's debts were paid when she acted in obedience to the Word of the Prophet. Our Salvation was bought by the obedience of our Saviour. We are instructed to teach our Disciples to obey.

# 7

# CAREFULNESS

**Definition:**

Carefulness is that considered approach we apply to our words, actions, deeds and thoughts, especially as we consider how it might advance or tarnish the Kingdom of God.

**Scriptures:**

> Matthew 16:6 (NIV)
> "6 "Be careful," Jesus said to them. "Be on your guard against the yeast of the Pharisees and Sadducees.""

> Colossians 4:5-6 (NIV)
> "5 Be wise in the way you act toward outsiders; make the most of every opportunity. 6 Let your conversation be always full of grace, seasoned with salt, so that you may know how to answer everyone.""

Ephesians 5:15 (NIV), Romans 12:17 (NIV), 1 Corinthians 8:9 (NIV)

## Characteristic explained:

Carefulness is the practice of applying care, caution and considera-tion to one's words, actions, deeds and thoughts, as well as taking care as to what one exposes oneself to. One the one hand it is an applica-tion of care over how we conduct ourselves and how our conduct might have a negative bearing on our confession of faith. The care and caution are applied as to not put the Gospel at risk of being slan-dered as a result of our conduct. On the other hand watchfulness, alertness and circumspection is applied as to what we expose ourselves to: in particular erroneous teachings, negative and toxic people, and unbecoming relationships.

## Life Application:

1. We value the teaching of Jesus when we apply care as to how we live, and how our conduct could be helpful to people, especially weak people, in believing in Him.

2. We value carefulness when we take care of what we listen to, whose teachings and doctrines we expose ourselves to, and the toxic relational environments we submit ourselves to.

Take care of your conduct daily, and take care as to the influ-encers you allow into your life. Bad company corrupts good morals.

# 8

## COMPASSION

**Definition:**

Compassion is the feeling of sorrow or pity for someone, and expressed by showing them kindness, mercy, sympathy or tenderness.

**Scriptures:**

> 1 Peter 3:8 "Finally, be ye all of one mind, having compassion one of another, love as brethren, be pitiful, be courteous:""
>
> Exodus 33:19 (NIV) "19 And the Lord said, "I will cause all my goodness to pass in front of you, and I will proclaim my name, the Lord, in your presence. I will have mercy on whom I will have mercy, and I will have compassion on whom I will have compassion.""

Psalms 116:5 (NIV) "5 The Lord is gracious and righteous; our God is full of compassion."

Exodus 22:26-27 (NIV), Psalms 86:15 (NIV), Matthew 9:36 (NIV), Colossians 3:12 (NIV), Philippians 2:1-2 (NIV)

**Characteristic explained:**

What we learnt about the Nature and Character of God, from the beginning, was His great Compassion for His people. On numerous occasions we see His love and Compassion expressed towards His people. Compassion is the show of sympathy, concern and empathy towards others in their distress or shortcomings. To be Compassionate is being kind-hearted and concerned with care for those around us. Compassion is showing consideration for the needs and care of others. We can see this compassionate care in the life of Christ expressed towards people on a number of occasions. He expressed it when He observed that they were like sheep without a Shepherd. He had compassion on the people when they were with Him for a few days without eating. He was concerned for their welfare. In the Apostle Paul's address to the Church in Philippi he exhorted them, through their union with Christ, to be "like-minded" and "have the same love" that they were comforted with through their union with Christ.

**Life Application:**

We value our relationship and union with Christ by walking in His footsteps, and desiring to live and be like Him. One of the ways in which we give credence to this union with Christ is by being compassionate. Take time to show kind-heartedness and care towards people around you on a daily basis. Take time to look for the challenges people face around you. May the challenges people face move us with the same compassion Christ is moved to help us in our weaknesses. Show concern, sympathy and understanding for the weaknesses people face daily. One of the most powerful ways in which we can show our true compassion, like Christ, is to help people in their weaknesses. See how you can help and assist people wherever you find yourself. *Take time to care and be kind.*

# PART III

# ASSIMILATION SHEET

**Spiritual Discipline: Worship**

1. What Scripture expresses God's desire for worshippers? _____
   _____
   _____

2. What is Worship? _____

   _____

3. In your own words describe what it means to self-surrender in Worship? _____

   _____
   _____

4. How will you make time to worship more?

   _____

5. What prepares us to enjoy the most fulfilling times in Worship?

   _____
   _____

## Values of the Kingdom of God

6. *"Servanthood"* is a Kingdom Value. Why is Servanthood such a huge Kingdom Value? _____

_____

_____

7. How will you define "loyalty" as a Kingdom Value?

_____

_____

_____

8. How can you be more *"Obedient"*?

_____

_____

_____

9. What does it mean to be *"Grateful"*?

_____

_____

_____

10. How can you be more *"Compassionate"*?

_____

_____

_____

# WEEK SEVEN

# PART I

## SPIRITUAL DISCIPLINE - SIMPLICITY

# 1

## SIMPLICITY

Jesus taught His Disciples on *the Spiritual Discipline of Simplicity.* Simplicity is the discipline of living contently with the least possible, and intentionally storing up treasures in Heaven with what is in hand. Jesus encouraged His Disciples to live simple lives without laying up earthly treasures.

> *"Simplicity is the discipline of living contently with the least possible, and intentionally storing up treasures in Heaven with what is in hand."*

The early Church lived such simple lives. We see that they sold their lands and houses and had everything in common. They laid their treasures at the feet of the Apostles, thus laying up treasures in Heaven. Their treasures were laid up in Kingdom Advancing pursuits. When He sent out His Disciples, He sent them out with a few simple instructions in Matthew 10. They were not to take with them a purse or extra sets of clothing. This is truly living a simple life.

> Matthew 10:9-10 (NIV) "⁹ "Do not get any gold or silver
> or copper to take with you in your belts— ¹⁰ no bag
> for the journey or extra shirt or sandals or a staff,
> for the worker is worth his keep."

**Our hearts show where our treasures are**

When Jesus taught His Disciples on the mountain, He encouraged them to lay up for themselves treasures in heaven, rather than accumulating treasures for themselves here on earth.

> Matthew 6:19-21 (NKJV) 19 "Do not lay up for
> yourselves treasures on earth, where moth and rust
> destroy and where thieves break in and steal; 20
> but lay up for yourselves treasures in heaven,
> where neither moth nor rust destroys and where
> thieves do not break in and steal. 21 For where your
> treasure is, there your heart will be also."

**What does it mean to "lay up for yourselves treasures in heaven?"**

*It primarily means to intentionally, invest generously into Kingdom Advancing missions.* Now this is not your tithe, which belongs to God, and we are instructed to return it to God in the local church where we are in fellowship. This *"laying up for yourselves"* of treasures is above and beyond the tithe. This giving, spending and sowing of your money should reflect that your heart, and treasure, is in advancing God's Kingdom. Every time we give towards missions, support the poor and needy, looking after widows and the elderly, we lay up treasures in Heaven.

> Matthew 19:21 (NIV) "²¹ Jesus answered, "If you want to
> be perfect, go, sell your possessions and give to the
> poor, and you will have treasure in heaven. Then
> come, follow me."

### Missions require treasures

Advancing the Kingdom of God among the poor requires a lot of money, both in providing in primary life supplies for local poor people, as well as providing support for those who work among them to uplift them through Discipleship materials to build disciple-making churches. Where we put our treasures is where our hearts will be also.

### Contentment is essential to Simplicity

The Apostle Paul speaks about contentment. In a simple way, to be content is to be disciplined in "*Simplicity,*" or living simply.

> Philippians 4:11 (NKJV) "11 Not that I speak in regard to need, for I have learned in whatever state I am, to be content:"

> 1 Timothy 6:6-8 (NKJV) "6 Now godliness with contentment is great gain. 7 For we brought nothing into this world, and it is certain we can carry nothing out. 8 And having food and clothing, with these we shall be content."

The early church modelled this discipline, and we read about them practicing "*simplicity*" frequently.

### Jesus practised Simplicity

> Matthew 8:20 (NIV) "20. Jesus replied, "Foxes have dens and birds have nests, but the Son of Man has no place to lay his head."

∾

### Jesus taught simplicity to His Disciples

When Jesus sent His Disciples out, He taught them this essential discipline of Simplicity. He taught them not to take gold, silver or copper with them. He taught them that the worker is worthy of his wages and that the Lord will provide for them wherever they go to share the Gospel.

> Matthew 10:9-10 (NIV) "9. Do not get any gold or silver or copper to take with you in your belts – 10. No bag for the journey or extra shirt or sandals or a staff, for the worker is worth his keep."

> Matthew 19:21 (NIV) "21. Jesus answered, "If you want to be perfect, go, sell your possessions and give to the poor, and you will have treasure in heaven. Then come, follow me.""

### The Church in Acts 2 practised Simplicity

When we look into what the early church did that enabled them to impact their world so effectively, we see that it is these practices and disciplines that spoke loudly to the world around them. Practicing Simplicity in many ways is something contra-cultural around the world, most people drive and aspire to accumulate more thing, not give or share things.

The early church practiced sharing and giving, two key essential heart attitudes in developing a kingdom culture.

> Acts 2:44-45 (NIV) "44. All the believers were together and had everything I common. 45. They sold property and possessions to give to anyone who had need."

Acts 4:32 (NIV) "32. All the believers were one in heart and mind. No one claimed that any of their possessions was their own, but they shared everything they had."

Acts 4:34-35 (NIV) "34. That there were no needy persons among them. For from time to time those who owned land and houses sold them, brought the money from the sales 35. And put it at the apostles' feet, and it was distributed to anyone who had need."

Practicing the discipline of simplicity is to make a concerted effort to store up treasures in Heaven, and to share what you have with those in the Household of Faith.

# PART II

## VALUES OF THE KINGDOM OF GOD

## 2

# CARING

**Definition:**

Caring is being thoughtful, sympathetic and lovingly helpful towards others, especially considering their cares, burdens and concerns.

**Scriptures:**

> Galatians 6:2 (NIV) "2 *Carry each other's burdens*, and in this way, you will fulfill the law of Christ."

> 1 Peter 5:2-3 (NIV) 2 *Be shepherds of God's flock* that is under your care, watching over them—not because you must, but because you are willing, as God wants you to be; not pursuing dishonest gain, but eager to serve; 3 not lording it over those entrusted to you, but *being examples* to the flock.

> 1 Timothy 5:4 (NIV), John 21:16 (NIV)

**Characteristic explained:**

Being caring is being mindful, considerate and helpful to others. Being Caring is to be lovingly concerned for the welfare of others. To be caring is to be sensitive to the needs and cares of others, and to treat them with compassion. One of the characteristics Jesus desired His Disciples to have was to *"take care"* of His sheep. To put it into the Words of Paul to Timothy, to *"take care"* is to put our religion into practice. We do what we value. Well, one of those true values in the Kingdom of God is to take care of those around you, and under your care.

**Life Application:**

We show care **firstly,** when we take note of the cares, concerns and burdens of people around us, especially those entrusted to our care. **Secondly,** we take care, when we do something about it, by showing love, being helpful and assisting. To be caring is to be mindful and considerate, in a way that shows those concerned, that you really care. We take care when we carry each other's burdens. One of the ways is, to relief the burden from a working, single parent, by offering to look after their children, to enable them to go and work, enabling them to earn a wage without having to add more pressure of having to pay for childcare. Another way is to assist with providing temporary care for people with ageing parents. Every time we step up to meet the needs of others, especially when we've taken the time to notice their distress and need of help, we honour God by providing care. Take care of each other, and carry each other's burdens, and in this way fulfill the way of love.

## 3

# CONFIDENCE

**Definition:**

Confidence is the trust and faith you have in someone or something. It is a strong belief and feeling of certainty with which you do things.

**Scriptures:**

> Philippians 1:6 (NIV) "6 *being confident of this*, that he who began a good work in you will carry it on to completion until the day of Christ Jesus."

> 2 Corinthians 3:4 (NIV) "4 *Such confidence we have through Christ before God.*"

> Ephesians 3:12 (NIV), Hebrews 4:16 (NIV), Hebrews 3:14 (NIV), Hebrews 3:6 (NIV), Hebrews 10:19 (NIV), Hebrews 10:35 (NIV), Hebrews 11:1 (NIV), Philippians 1:6 (NIV)

**Characteristic explained:**

God is the source of confidence, and as we place our indisputable trust and faith in Him, He works this confidence in us to do extraordinary things. Hebrews 11 verse one starts by saying: *"Now faith is confidence..."* Confidence is to have faith in someone or something. *Confidence is that assurance* of how sure you are, to *the extent that you will act on the confidence you have*, especially as it relates to our faith and confidence in what God said in His Word, and therefore we act upon His Word. *Confidence is expressed by the certainty with which you act* and do things. Confidence is that self-reliant, self-confident act in assurance of faith. In other words, *you do because you are convinced* and *assured*.

**Life Application:**

Faith is confidence in what we hope for to be true. We give expression to our faith by the confident way upon which we act upon the Words and Instructions of the Bible. There is a direct correlation between the faith we have and the confidence with which we carry ourselves. Never lose your confidence in the things you've become assured of, especially about your faith in God and His Word. Act in confidence. May our confidence show others how strong your faith in God really is.

# 4

## STEADFASTNESS

**Definition:**

Steadfastness is the inner assertiveness to be firmly fixed and focused on doing what you purposed to do. It is the ability to be constant and unchanging in your course of faith and action.

**Scriptures:**

> Matthew 10:22 (NIV) "22 You will be hated by everyone because of me, but *the one who stands firm to the end will be saved*."

> Matthew 24:12-13 (NIV) "12 Because of the increase of wickedness, the love of most will grow cold, 13 but the one who stands firm to the end will be saved."

1 Corinthians 15:58 (NIV) "58 Therefore, my dear brothers and sisters, *stand firm. Let nothing move you.* Always give yourselves fully to the work of the Lord, because you know that your labour in the Lord is not in vain.

2 Thessalonians 2:15 (NIV), Hebrews 10:23 (NIV), Isaiah 26:3 (NIV)

## Characteristic explained:

Steadfastness is that loyal and firm commitment to keep firmly to your beliefs. Steadfastness is to be uncompromisingly firm in one's convictions. Steadfastness is that persistent, loyal resoluteness to stay the course. Firmness speaks of consistency and dependability. Firmness is expressed in us being inflexible, uncompromising rigid, and determined to hold on to what we belief, and the principles we determined to live our lives by.

## Life Application:

### How do we give expression to this Kingdom value?

**Firstly,** by subscribing and determining to learn, adopt and live by the values and principles of the Bible.

**Secondly,** we give expression to Firmness or Steadfastness by intentionally putting the principles and values, of the Biblically learnt values, before our preferences, habitual reactions or responses.

**Thirdly,** by developing a resoluteness, because of how it pleases God when we stand by the values of the Kingdom of God, to maintain and be loyal to your decision to do things according to what the Bible teaches. God desires us to be pre-determined and resolute in our following of Him. I pray that we will be those who stand uncompromisingly firm in our decisions to follow the teachings of Jesus.

# CONTENTMENT

**Definition:**

Contentment is the pre-positioning and determination of being satisfied and pleased regardless of the circumstances you might find yourself in. Contentment is the satisfaction with one's current state.

**Scriptures:**

> Matthew 6:25 (NIV) "25 "Therefore I tell you, *do not worry about your life, what you will eat or drink; or about your body, what you will wear*. Is not life more than food, and the body more than clothes?
>
> 1 Timothy 6:6 (NIV) "6 But *godliness with contentment is great gain*."
>
> 1 Timothy 6:8 (NIV), Philippians 4:11-12 (NIV)

**Characteristic explained:**

Contentment is a learnt value, like every other Value. To be content is to be satisfied with what you have. It is a pre-determination that if you have food, something to drink, and clothes to wear, that you have everything you need to live, and with that in mind, to be grateful for everything else beyond that.

**Life Application:**

### How content am I?

People love to be around people who are content with what they have. There is a balance to strike between being content with what you have and what you don't have. Many people live so focused on what they don't have that they always present themselves, not willingly, as deprived people. I love to be around people who are satisfied with what they have. This does not mean that they don't aspire for more, or for bigger and better things, no, their satisfaction and contentment outweigh the bearing of their wants and desires. May we live content with what we have, with that which our Father in Heaven blessed us with.

## 6

## TEACHABLE

**Definition:**

To be Teachable requires the willingness to learn and be changed and transformed in condition, character, form or appearance, especially into the likeness of Christ.

**Scripture:**

> Matthew 11:29 (NIV) 29 Take my yoke upon you and learn from me, for I am gentle and humble in heart, and you will find rest for your souls.

> John 6:45 (NIV) 45 It is written in the Prophets: 'They will all be taught by God.'[a] Everyone who has heard the Father and learned from him comes to me."
>
> Romans 12:2, Colossians 3:10 (NIV), Ephesians 4:22-24 (NIV)

**Characteristic explained:**

We are Teachable when we open our hearts to be renewed in our minds. Only a commitment to being renewed in the spirit of your mind will ensure a lifetime of being teachable. Transformation takes place when we determinately put off our old self, and determinately put on the new self. We become what we pursue in our minds and in our hearts. For us as Believers it is the determination to get rid of the old worldly nature and to constantly open ourselves to be renewed our minds with the things of God. In each of these instances where we read about the process of Transformation, it is really a matter of putting the things that was taught into practice, and that requires us to remain Teachable. The more we willingly put things into the forefront of our minds, the more we change and transform.

**Life Application:**

I love the way the writer to the Romans puts it. To be Teachable is about a constant decision to change, and a determination to not conform to the pattern of this world. To be teachable requires us to transform. Conforming is the result of simply accepting the ways of the world as the norm and you simply comply, however, on the other hand, transformation come when we are teachable and actively engage in embracing the values of the Kingdom of God as our own, and practicing them. Ask yourself the question, in every decision that confronts our moral standing, whether we are conforming or transforming. I saw this characteristic in one of my Pastor's, their ability to adopt new ways of doing things, and adapting to changing circumstances as well as flowing with the way the Spirit works within the Church. One simple example was with the way in which he responded to the operation of the gifts of the Holy Spirit within his churches.

The question remains:

- How Teachable am I?
- How open am I to receive correction or instruction?"

# DEFERENCE

**Definition:**

Deference is the considered and thoughtful action of living an exemplary life with the expressed purpose of leading others to Christ through your way of living in constant reference to Him and His Word.

**Scriptures:**

> Matthew 5:16 (NIV) "16 In the same way, *let your light shine before others, that they may see your good deeds and glorify your Father in heaven.*"

> John 5:30 (NIV) "30 By myself I can do nothing; I judge only as I hear, and my judgment is just, for *I seek not to please myself but him who sent me.*"

1 Corinthians 9:22 (NIV), I Corinthians 10:33, James 4:15 (NIV), Romans 14:13 (NIV), Ephesians 5:1-2 (NIV)

## Characteristic explained:

Deference is the expression of awe and adoration for someone or something, with the expressed purpose of leading others into the same allegiance. Deference refers to the way we show others who we have a high regard for. Deference is the showing of esteemed respect and regard for a person and His teachings or views. Deference living is the expressed value of living in strong reference to the Bible, and is expressed by one's submission to it. Our lives should strongly reflect our allegiance to the Bible and especially the teachings of Jesus. Deference living is living a life that point people to Christ, and shows others that we live in submission to Him and His Word. Jesus modelled this to us throughout His earthly ministry. When tempted by the Devil, He referred to the Scriptures. When questioned about His Authority, He pointed to the One who sent Him and whose instructions and Will He fulfil. Deference means to show submission, allegiance and compliance, but also reverence, awe and regard. For us as Believers it is the constant using of every opportunity to point people to the One, we adore and value as the Supreme Leader and Authority in our lives, like Jesus did.

## Life Application:

A value is only valued if practiced and observed in one's daily life. A good question to ask this week is:

*How can I, through my words and deeds, show others that I greatly value and honour God and His Word in my life?*

*We do what we value.* Our values are seen and observed by what we say and do. Every time we refer to the Bible as our point of reference for guidance, we practice deference. Every time we say: *"If the*

*Lord willing*," we practice deference, and give expression to our high regard for living in Favour with Him. Every time we give honour to the Lord when things turn out for good, or when something good happens, we practice deference. It is the active giving of honour, and expressing gratitude to the Lord in every situation that shows others that we truly value God, His Son, the Holy Spirit and the Word, in our lives. Now, let's think again on ways in which we can actively bring honour to God through our words and deeds today.

# 8

## DILIGENCE

**Definition:**

Diligence is the paying of careful and unceasing attention to doing things well. Diligence is developed in us by paying attention and being conscientious in everything we do.

**Scriptures:**

> John 4:34 (NIV) "34 "My food," said Jesus, "is *to do the will of him who sent me* and *to finish his work*."

> Colossians 3:23 "And *whatsoever ye do, do it heartily, as to the Lord*, and not unto men.

> 1 Thessalonians 4:11-12 (NIV), Ecclesiastes 9:10 (NIV), Colossians 3:22-24 (NIV)

**Characteristic explained:**

Diligence is the practice of careful and attentive thoroughness. To be diligent is to be persistently meticulous. It is to be tirelessly working at things until it is done. Jesus was diligent in finishing the tasks set before Him. He modelled working tirelessly and diligently to seek and save the lost and to finish the course of His Life with excellence. He was diligent to the end. God desires that we apply this same endurance of diligence to our work ethics. We need to finish what we start. We are diligent not only in completing tasks, but in completing them with the right attitude as well. Diligent people always do that extra bit. You are diligent when you apply yourself to every task wholeheartedly, and with such devotion that it attracts the respect of outsiders.

**Life Application:**

We all have tasks to do today. These might be formal required tasks, like doing your job for which you are paid, or informal casually required tasks like doing the dishes or laundry. The thing to consider is whether I am giving credence to this value in my approach to the tasks at hand.

- Diligence requires the right attitude in that I do everything as unto the Lord.
- Diligence also requires me to do things to the best of my abilities, not half-hearted or just to get it over and done.
- Diligence requires a constant focus on who I am doing things for.
- It requires sincerity of heart and reverence for the Lord.

Let us earnestly consider the diligence we apply to the tasks before us today, and every day, regardless of who we perform them for.

# PART III

# ASSIMILATION SHEET

## Spiritual Discipline: Simplicity

1. Did Jesus teach His Disciples on Simplicity? _____
   If Yes, What did Jesus teach His Disciples on Simplicity? _____
   _____
   _____

2. What does it mean to "lay up for yourselves treasures in heaven?" _____
   _____

3. Define Simplicity? _____
   _____
   _____

4. What is an essential of living Simply? _____
   _____
   _____

5. How did the early Church practice Simplicity, and give Scriptures to back this up? _____
   _____

## Values of the Kingdom of God

6. *"Caring"* is a Kingdom Value. Why is Caring such an amazing Kingdom Value? _____

_____

_____

_____

7. Describe what it means to be Steadfast?

_____

_____

_____

_____

8. How can you be more *"Content"*?

_____

_____

_____

_____

9. What does it mean to be *"Deferent"*?

_____

_____

_____

_____

# WEEK EIGHT

# PART I

---

# SPIRITUAL DISCIPLINE - SERVANTHOOD

# 1

## SERVANTHOOD

Jesus taught His Disciples *the Spiritual Discipline of Servanthood*. If you have Kingdom advancing aspirations, it is best done along the pathway of service to your fellow man.

### Jesus modelled serving

One of the chief expressions of this discipline is through us following in the example of our Lord and Saviour, Jesus Christ, when He modelled to us on the washing of feet.

> Mark 9:35 (NKJV) "35 And He sat down, called the twelve, and said to them, "If anyone desires to be first, he shall be last of all and servant of all."

> John 13:14-17 (NKJV) "14 If I then, your Lord and Teacher, have washed your feet, you also ought to wash one another's feet. 15 For I have given you an example, that you should do as I have done to you. 16 Most assuredly, I say to you, a servant is not greater than his master; nor is he who is sent

greater than he who sent him. 17 If you know these
things, blessed are you if you do them."

Jesus modelled this in a number of ways. He served humanity by
His death and resurrection. He served His Disciples by giving them
the Words of Life. He laid His life down for His sheep. Serving is
giving yourself wholly for a cause. It is the applying of all your
mental, physical and emotional faculties for the cause of advancing
the Kingdom of God through our active engagement with people in
and out of the Kingdom of God.

> John 13:34 (KJV) "I give you a new commandment, That
> ye love one another as I have loved you"

From the Latin form of this commandment of Christ, we learn
that we should imitate His loving humility in the washing of the feet.

### We serve by working hard and diligent

We as Believers should be the most loyal, hardworking and
faithful people wherever we work. We represent a Kingdom, the
Kingdom of God, and the way we work reflects on the Kingdom we
represent.

> 2 Thessalonians 3:10" [10] For even when we were with
> you, we gave you this rule: "If a man will not work,
> he shall not eat.""

> Ephesians 6:5-6 (TPT) "⁵ Those who are employed
> should listen to their employers and obey their
> instructions with great respect and honor. Serve
> them with humility in your hearts as though you
> were working for the Master. ⁶ Always do what is
> right and not only when others are watching, so
> that you may please Christ as his servants by doing

his will. [7] Serve your employers wholeheartedly
and with love, as though you were serving Christ
and not men."

I love the way the Passion Translation puts it, because now people should associate with the language that was used in the original language. *Employees are those who don't work for themselves but are employed in the service of another.* During the time of the writing of the Bible, those who did not, or could not work to keep themselves sustained, submitted themselves to the employ of another, and therefor became their servants or in extreme circumstances became slaves. In simple terms of understanding, a "_____" is an "*employee*", and a "*Master*" is an "_____."

### Those who are employed should serve well.

**Believers should be:**
1. The *most obedient* employees,
2. The *most* _____ employees,
3. The *most loyal* employees,
4. The *humblest* employees,
5. The *most faithful* employees,
6. The *most* _____ employees, and
7. The *most serving* employees.

### Believers always represent the Kingdom of God.

Almost every single Scripture that addresses the responsibilities of "*slaves,*" or "*employees*" make the *direct connection* between our faith and the way we serve or work. It also directs the heart attitude with which we need to serve; "*as unto the Lord.*"

> 1 Timothy 6:1-2 (NIV) "[1] All who are under the yoke of
> slavery should consider their masters worthy of
> full respect, so that God's name and our teaching

may not be slandered. [2] Those who have believing masters should not show them disrespect just because they are fellow believers. Instead, they should serve them even better because their masters are dear to them as fellow believers and are devoted to the welfare of their slaves."

I Peter 2:18-20 (NIV) "[18] Slaves, in reverent fear of God submit yourselves to your masters, not only to those who are good and considerate, but also to those who are harsh. [19] For it is commendable if someone bears up under the pain of unjust suffering because they are conscious of God. [20] But how is it to your credit if you receive a beating for doing wrong and endure it? But if you suffer for doing good and you endure it, this is commendable before God."

Titus 2:9-10 (NIV) "[9] Teach slaves to be subject to their masters in everything, to try to please them, not to talk back to them, [10] and not to steal from them, but to show that they can be fully trusted, so that in every way they will make the teaching about God our Savior attractive."

**We serve by doing the good _____ God calls us to do.**

Ephesians 2:10 (NIV) "We are God's workmanship, created in Christ Jesus to do good works, which God prepared in advance for us to do!"

God prepared good works for us to do. By doing those deeds God calls us to do, we serve His purpose. In fact, God desires for us to use whatever gifts we have to serve others.

1 Peter 4:10-11 (NIV) "10 Each of you should use whatever gift you have received to serve others, as faithful stewards of God's grace in its various forms. 11 If anyone speaks, they should do so as one who speaks the very words of God. If anyone serves, they should do so with the strength God provides, so that in all things God may be praised through Jesus Christ. To him be the glory and the power for ever and ever. Amen."

Hebrews 6:10 (NIV) "10 God is not unjust; he will not forget your work and the love you have shown him as you have helped his people and continue to help them."

1 Corinthians 15:58 (NIV) "58 Therefore, my dear brothers and sisters, stand firm. Let nothing move you. Always give yourselves fully to the work of the Lord, because you know that your labor in the Lord is not in vain."

Romans 14:18 (NIV) "18 because anyone who serves Christ in this way is pleasing to God and receives human approval."

### Serve your way up!

Use whatever gifts you received to serve others. The greatest leaders in the Bible are those who served their leaders and subsequently succeeded them. We have the example of Joseph serving in the household of Pharaoh, and after serving him faithfully and well, Joseph got promoted to the second highest position and authority in Egypt. We also have the example of Joshua serving Moses as his attendant until God instructed Moses to appoint Joshua to succeed him. After Elisha served and followed in the footsteps of Elijah, he succeeded him as a prophet. David served Saul before succeeding him as King.

Serve your way into the anointing you desire upon your life. Seek and pursue opportunities where you may serve men and woman of God.

# PART II

# VALUES OF THE KINGDOM OF GOD

# TRUSTWORTHINESS

**Definition:**

*Trustworthiness is truthfulness and faithfulness combined.* This is a rewarded characteristic of Believers. Believers are known for their trustworthiness, truthfulness and faithfulness.

**Scriptures:**

> Matthew 25:21 (NIV) "21 "His master replied, 'Well done, good and faithful servant! You have been faithful with a few things; I will put you in charge of many things. Come and share your master's happiness!'

> 1 Timothy 6:20 (NIV) "20 Timothy, guard what has been entrusted to your care. Turn away from godless chatter and the opposing ideas of what is falsely called knowledge,"

1 Corinthians 4:2 (NIV) "2 Now it is required that those
who have been given a trust must prove faithful."

## Characteristic explained:

Trustworthiness is the practice of good stewardship over the gifts,
talents and resources we have. Trustworthiness is the practice of
honesty and reliability. Trustworthiness is defined by being
constantly dependably and responsible. Credibility is one of the key
characteristics of someone who is trustworthy. The extent to which
we take responsibility is seen in the way we treat the feelings and
possessions of others. Most people take care of their own things, but
rarely are people attentive to take care of the possessions of another.
In the Kingdom of God we embrace the fact that everything belongs
to God, and that we are purely entrusted steward of what belongs to
Him. For Believers, it is essential that we practice the taking of
responsibility and that we live to be worthy of more trust.

## Life Application:

The question therefor to ask oneself is:

- *Am I a constantly reliable person upon whom others can depend?*
- *Am I honest and credible?*
- *Do I take responsibility for things I do and are involved in?*

It should be our desire and intention to be people whom God can
trust with His most treasured Gifts. Take responsibility for your
actions, reactions and words today. Live, and conduct yourself in such
a way that it will show people that you are worthy of their trust. They
can depend on you since you are constantly reliable and dependable.

# 3

## GENTLENESS

**Definition:**

Gentleness is the ability to be patient and kind, and expressed by a continual compassionate leniency towards all people.

**Scriptures:**

> Matthew 11:29 (NIV) "29 Take my yoke upon you and learn from me, for I am gentle and humble in heart, and you will find rest for your souls."

> 2 Timothy 2:24 "And the servant of the Lord must not strive; but be gentle unto all men, apt to teach, and patient."

> Galatians 5:22-23 (NIV), Philippians 4:5 (NIV), Colossians 3:12-14 (NIV), 1 Timothy 6:11 (NIV)

**Characteristic explained:**

*Gentleness is the practice of tenderness.* Gentleness is practiced when we are calm and approach situations with kindness. Having a softer approach is prized as gentleness. God desires us to be gentle in our dealings with people, but also to be gentle in how we handle difficult and complex situations. One of the greatest expressions and examples of this was the way in which Jesus handled the woman who was caught in adultery. He had a gentler approach with her. Being gentle is to practice forbearance, to be gracious and determinately soft.

**Life Application:**

God desires that those who profess Him as Lord, in whom He deposited His Holy Spirit, will be gentle, and that their gentleness be seen and known to all.

The question to answer to yourself is:

- *Do I allow the gentleness of Christ to be made known to others around me?*
- *Am I intentionally, and thoughtfully gentle in difficult situations?*
- *How can I let my gentleness be more visible to others, as Christ want me to be?*
- *What does the gentleness of Christ look like, and am I learning from Him on how to be gentle and kind?*

The thoughtful and considered answering to these questions in my life will most certainly leave me gentler in nature and conduct.

# 4

## DISCERNMENT

**Definition:**

Discernment is the ability to distinguish between right and wrong, between what is more expedient or not, and what is best. Discernment is also the ability to see the difference between things and to understand clearly the distinction between thoughts, ideas and concepts.

**Scriptures:**

> Philippians 1:10 (NIV) "10 so that you may be able to discern what is best and may be pure and blameless for the day of Christ,"

> Philippians 1:9-11 (NIV), Hebrews 5:14 (NIV), Ezekiel 44:23 (NIV), Psalms 119:125 (NIV), 1 Corinthians 12:10 (NIV)

**Characteristic explained:**

*Discernment is the ability to make sensitive decisions based on sound and selective judgement.* Discernment is the applied ability to judge for yourself between things. The Bible teaches that this is both an applied and developing value, as well as a gift God gives us, especially concerning spiritual things. Our constant application of this value will help us greatly to make wise and enduring decisions. Discernment is the ability to distinguish between what is good and what is evil and to value making a choice for the good. Discernment deals particularly with making good, positive and up building choices. People who don't apply discernment to their lives live carelessly and are often surprised when the impact of their careless and thoughtless actions and words become known.

Life Application:

We all face the making of decisions between good and evil every day. Applying this value is to recognize whether we are deciding for good rather than for evil. Hebrews 5 tells us that it is an acquired value by practicing to choose good over evil. We mature in our faith when we apply this skill diligently.

It is beneficial to ask oneself:

- *Is it helpful?*
- *Is it going to impact people positively?*
- *Will people be built up through this decision?*
- *Will it be beneficial?*
- *Is this a positive decision?*

Anything other than a positive and affirmative answer to any of these probing questions will leave you erring in applying discernment. Mature people apply great discernment to their lives. Their ability to discern makes them people with understanding.

# 5

# TRUTHFULNESS

**Definition:**

Truthfulness is the ability to speak and act in an honest, open, just, reliable and righteous way.

**Scripture:**

> Ephesians 4:25 "Wherefore putting away lying, speak every man truth with his Neighbour: for we are members one of another."

> Psalms 15:2 (NIV) "2 The one whose walk is blameless, who does what is righteous, who speaks the truth from their heart;"

> Proverbs 22:20-21, Matthew 22:16 (NIV), 1 Corinthians 4:17 (NIV)

**Characteristic explained:**

*To be truthful is to be honest, straight, open, true and reliable.* To be truthful is to speak reliable facts as they are. Truthfulness is one of the key essential values of someone who hold high integrity and character. Truthful people speak ingeniously open and straight. They say things as they are and not as people want to hear them, neither do they add their own slant to it. Truthfulness also relates to one's actions, that they are consistent with the faith and integrity you profess. Truthful people live with integrity to their moral standing and faith.

**Life Application:**

We are truthful when we speak what is true and reliable. We are truthful when we are honest and open. We are truthful when we uphold facts with integrity of conscience. May we always tell things in a way that is reliable and true to the facts. Truthfulness should be reflected in the way we live before all people, and in all circumstances. Truthful people live the same, and speak the same at church as what they live and speak at home. Whenever we say something, we should ask ourselves whether it is the truth, consistent with the facts? We should consider our actions and behaviour before all men, as to whether they truly reflect who we are and what we stand for. Live in such a way that you can maintain your peace at all times.

# GENEROSITY

**Definition:**

Generosity is the ability to be unselfish with a readiness to share and to give freely.

**Scriptures:**

> Matthew 10:8 (NIV) "8 Heal the sick, raise the dead, cleanse those who have leprosy, drive out demons. Freely you have received; freely give."

> Matthew 25:34-36 (NIV) "34 "Then the King will say to those on his right, 'Come, you who are blessed by my Father; take your inheritance, the kingdom prepared for you since the creation of the world. 35 For I was hungry and you gave me something to eat, I was thirsty and you gave me something to drink, I was a stranger and you invited me in, 36 I

needed clothes and you clothed me, I was sick and
you looked after me, I was in prison and you came
to visit me.'"

Acts 20:35 (NIV) "35 In everything I did, I showed you
that by this kind of hard work we must help the
weak, remembering the words the Lord Jesus
himself said: 'It is more blessed to give than to
receive."

2 Corinthians 8:2-4 (NIV), 2 Corinthians 9:6 (NIV), 2
Corinthians 9:11, 13 (NIV)

## Characteristic explained:

*Generosity is a way of expressing gratitude* for the gifts and blessings
we share in life, *by giving back.* Generosity is *the act of kindness by
being open-handed* and liberal in our giving of kindness. Generosity is
expressed when we give cheerfully. Generosity is expressed in everything we do, whether that be in being gracious, compassionate,
loving or faithful, in fact, whatever we do, let us be generous in the
expression of our giving. Generosity is the expression of a heart attitude. Some people think that you have to be wealthy to be generous,
but I have seen more generosity among poor people than among the
wealthy. The example of the Macedonians shows us the true heart of
the generous spirit that they gave with joy, in spite of extreme
poverty.

## Life Application:

When we give ourselves, and of ourselves liberally then we are gener-
ous. Every time we show kindness unreservedly, we are generous.
Generosity is the opening of our heart to show and express kindness.
Generosity is shown when we heartily apply ourselves in every situa-

tion to see what we can do, and do it. Generous people give unreservedly! Generous people are Sowers, they value the seed they have, and they sow it. Search your heart and look for ways in which you could show generosity.

# 7

## KINDNESS

**Definition:**

Kindness is that generally warm-hearted, friendly and well-meaning interaction with others. Kindness is seen in the thoughtfulness and consideration with which we deal with people.

**Scriptures:**

> Ephesians 4:32 (NIV) "32 Be kind and compassionate to one another, forgiving each other, just as in Christ God forgave you."
> Colossians 3:12 (NIV) "12 Therefore, as God's chosen people, holy and dearly loved, clothe yourselves with compassion, kindness, humility, gentleness and patience."
> Galatians 5:22 (NIV) "22 But the fruit of the Spirit is love, joy, peace, forbearance, kindness, goodness, faithfulness,"

**Characteristic explained:**

The key characteristics of those who embrace *kindness is that they are considerate, caring, kind-hearted, and sympathetic in the way they deal with others.* Kindness is expressed by being gentle, thoughtful and humane in dealing with people.

**Life Application:**

The question we need to answer ourselves is:

- *How kind am I in my responses, both in gesture, action and words?*
- *Is the kindness I intend to show visible and observable by others, especially those to whom I intend to show and express kindness to?*

Make it a prepositioned intention to be kind and to pursue acts of kindness every day. The most recognizable international sign of Kindness is said to be that of an endearing and warm-hearted smile. Practice your smile, and offer a smile to people wherever you go. Pursue opportunities to show unexpected kindness and help to people wherever you can every day. Make it part of who you are.

# PART III

# ASSIMILATION SHEET

### Spiritual Discipline: Servanthood

1. Did Jesus teach His Disciples on Servanthood? _____
   If Yes, What did Jesus teach His Disciples on Servanthood? ___

   _____

   _____

   _____

2. Name Seven ways in which Believers can excel in Serving? __

   _____

   _____

   _____

   _____

### Values of the Kingdom of God

3. Why is *"Trustworthiness"* so valued as an amazing Kingdom Value? _____

4. Describe the value of "*Gentleness*"?

_____

_____

_____

5. How can you be more "*Discerning*"?

_____

_____

_____

6. What does it mean to be "*Truthful*"?

_____

_____

_____

7. How can you be more "*Generous*"?

_____

_____

_____

8. What does it mean to be "Kind"?

_____

_____

_____

# WEEK NINE

# PART I

---

# SPIRITUAL DISCIPLINE - WITNESSING

# 1

## WITNESSING

Jesus taught His Disciples *the Spiritual Discipline of Witnessing* when He first taught them on the mountain. He said to them that they were *"Light"* and *"Salt"* and that they should let their *"light so shine before others that they may see your good deeds and glorify your Father in Heaven."* This is a clear directive to be a witness for the Light of the World.

**Witnessing requires a commitment to both be a "_____" and "_____."**

> Matthew 5:13-16 (NIV) [13] "You are the salt of the earth. But if the salt loses its saltiness, how can it be made salty again? It is no longer good for anything, except to be thrown out and trampled underfoot. [14] "You are the light of the world. A town built on a hill cannot be hidden. [15] Neither do people light a lamp and put it under a bowl. Instead they put it on its stand, and it gives light to everyone in the house. [16] In the same way, let your light shine

before others, that they may see your good
deeds and glorify your Father in heaven."

To be a *"light"* means that we commit to go on public display as
an example for others to see the *"Light"* of Christ shining brightly in
our lives through the *"good deeds"* they observe in and through our
lives. To be *"Salt"* requires us to live worthily, upholding the values of
the Kingdom of God through our high-principled conduct. On the
other hand, to be a witness also requires us to share the Word of God
by mouth.

**Witnessing requires a commitment to "_____" the Good News.**

During the parting moments before Jesus Ascended to Heaven,
He gave His Disciples the *"Great Commission."* The Great Commis-
sion requires us to *"go"* out into the whole world and *"preach"* the
Good News about Jesus Christ and *"Disciple"* them into obedient
Followers of Jesus Christ.

> Mark 16:15 (NIV) "15 He said to them, 'Go into all the
> world and preach the gospel to all creation.'"

> Mark 16:20 (NIV) "20 Then the disciples went out and
> preached everywhere, and the Lord worked with
> them and confirmed his word by the signs that
> accompanied it."

**Witnessing requires a commitment to both "preach" and
"_____."**

Jesus not only requires His Followers to *"go into all the world and
preach the gospel,"* He also requires them to *"disciple"* those whose
hearts are opened and who respond to the Gospel message that is
preached.

Matthew 28:19-20 (NIV) "19 Therefore go and make
disciples of all nations, baptizing them in the name
of the Father and of the Son and of the Holy Spirit,
20 and teaching them to obey everything I have
commanded you. And surely, I am with you always,
to the very end of the age."

*The church in Acts did exactly that; they preached and made
disciples.* Jesus instructed us to *"preach"* the gospel and to *"teach"* our
disciples what He taught us. The early church did just that. It was this
broader embracing of the Final Instruction the Lord gave His Disciples that gave precedence to it becoming the *"Great Commission."*

Acts 11:19-21 (NIV) "19 Now those who had been
scattered by the persecution that broke out when
Stephen was killed traveled as far as Phoenicia,
Cyprus and Antioch, spreading the word only
among Jews. 20 Some of them, however, men from
Cyprus and Cyrene, went to Antioch and began to
speak to Greeks also, telling them the good news
about the Lord Jesus. 21 The Lord's hand was with
them, and a great number of people believed and
turned to the Lord."

Acts 11:25-26 (NIV) 25 Then Barnabas went to Tarsus to
look for Saul, 26 and when he found him, he
brought him to Antioch. So for a whole year
Barnabas and Saul met with the church and taught
great numbers of people. The disciples were called
Christians first at Antioch.

We see this pattern replicated on many accounts in the Acts of the
Apostles. It is no wonder that the early church grew exponentially. I
believe, and see, that we will experience the same impact and transformation of nations as what the Apostles and the early church expe-

rienced, if we embrace again, as the body of Christ, as Believers, the "Great Commission" as our mission. We will cover the earth with the Good News of Jesus Christ.

### How will they believe without someone telling them?

> Romans 10:14-15 (NIV 1984) 14 How, then, can they call on the one they have not believed in? And how can they believe in the one of whom they have not heard? And how can they hear without someone preaching to them? 15 And how can they preach unless they are sent? As it is written, "How beautiful are the feet of those who bring good news!"

### Jesus modelled preaching and discipling

Jesus started His earthly ministry by doing exactly that; He preached a Message of Repentance everywhere he went. John the Baptist also started His ministry by preaching. The Apostles did the same. It is no wonder that they were able to reach their entire world with the Gospel since they went out, preached, and bore witness, and discipled the new Believers.

> Matthew 3:1-2 (NIV) "1 In those days John the Baptist came, preaching in the wilderness of Judea 2 and saying, "Repent, for the kingdom of heaven has come near.""

> Matthew 4:17 (NIV) "17 From that time on Jesus began to preach, "Repent, for the kingdom of heaven has come near.""

As a result of this preaching Jesus found His first Disciples. We see this process modelled by Jesus in the Gospel of Luke. First Jesus preached, and then performed a miracle, and then Peter bowed his knees to Jesus and followed Him as His Disciple.

> Luke 5:1 (NIV) "1 One day as Jesus was standing by the
> Lake of Gennesaret, the people were crowding
> around him and listening to the word of God."

Jesus preached the Word of God next to the Lake of Gennesaret. It is here that He meets Peter, Andrew, James and John, the owners of two fishing trawlers.

> Luke 5:4-6 (NIV) "4 When he had finished speaking, he
> said to Simon, 'Put out into deep water, and let
> down the nets for a catch.'"5 Simon answered,
> 'Master, we've worked hard all night and haven't
> caught anything. But because you say so, I will let
> down the nets.' 6 When they had done so, they
> caught such a large number of fish that their nets
> began to break."

Jesus performed a miracle that astounded them. One of the consistent elements we witness in the work of the early church was their passionate obedience to "*preach*" Jesus, "*perform miracles, signs and wonders,*" and "disciple". In the midst of severe persecution the church advanced and even won the hostile Roman Empire.

> Luke 5:8-9 (NIV) "8 When Simon Peter saw this, he fell
> at Jesus' knees and said, 'Go away from me, Lord; I
> am a sinful man!' 9 For he and all his companions
> were astonished at the catch of fish they had
> taken."

On a number of occasions we see this same pattern of ministry replicated as well; Preach, miracles, repentance and people becoming Followers.

Luke 5:10-11 (NIV) 10 "...Then Jesus said to Simon,
'Don't be afraid; from now on you will fish for
people.' 11 So they pulled their boats up on shore,
left everything and followed him."

These first Disciples of the Lord witnesses firsthand a miracle, the impact of which impacted them so much that Peter fell to his knees and "confessed" that he was a sinner. The impact of us "preaching" or speaking the Word of God should result in people putting their faith in Jesus.

**Peter preached, performed _____ and discipled wherever he went**

The Apostle Peter was such an example of practicing this Spiritual Discipline right from the onset of the Church's Foundation. He is the one who stood up in the Day of Pentecost and preached that message that saw 3000 people coming to Christ.

Acts 2:14 (NIV) Peter Addresses the Crowd 14 Then
Peter stood up with the Eleven, raised his voice and
addressed the crowd: "Fellow Jews and all of you
who live in Jerusalem, let me explain this to you;
listen carefully to what I say."

Acts 2:22 (NIV) "22 Fellow Israelites, listen to this: Jesus
of Nazareth was a man accredited by God to you by
miracles, wonders and signs, which God did
among you through him, as you yourselves know."

Acts 2:31-33 (NIV) 31 Seeing what was to come, he spoke
of the resurrection of the Messiah, that he was not
abandoned to the realm of the dead, nor did his
body see decay. 32 God has raised this Jesus to life,
and we are all witnesses of it. 33 Exalted to the right

hand of God, he has received from the Father the promised Holy Spirit and has poured out what you now see and hear."

Acts 2:36-41 (NIV) 36 "Therefore let all Israel be assured of this: God has made this Jesus, whom you crucified, both Lord and Messiah." 37 When the people heard this, they were cut to the heart and said to Peter and the other apostles, "Brothers, what shall we do?" 38 Peter replied, "Repent and be baptized, every one of you, in the name of Jesus Christ for the forgiveness of your sins. And you will receive the gift of the Holy Spirit. 39 The promise is for you and your children and for all who are far off—for all whom the Lord our God will call." 40 With many other words he warned them; and he pleaded with them, "Save yourselves from this corrupt generation." 41 Those who accepted his message were baptized, and about three thousand were added to their number that day."

On many other occasions we see the same pattern of witnessing being followed; miracles, preaching and people putting their faith in Jesus Christ. In the Acts of the Apostles, chapter three, we read about the Lame Beggar being healed, which was followed with an opportunity to share about Jesus of Nazareth. 5000 people came to the Lord as a result of that witnessing about the Lord Jesus being the Resurrected Christ and Messiah.

Acts 3:9-10 (NIV) "9 When all the people saw him walking and praising God, 10 they recognized him as the same man who used to sit begging at the temple gate called Beautiful, and they were filled with wonder and amazement at what had happened to him."

The focus of his message was clear: repent, that your sins might be wiped out, and that times of refreshing might come.

> Acts 3:19 (NIV) "19 Repent, then, and turn to God, so
> that your sins may be wiped out, that times of
> refreshing may come from the Lord,"

The impact of the Lord working with Peter as He brought witness of the Lord Jesus was incredible. First the Sadducees and Teachers of the Law was infuriated by Peter and John's message on the Resurrection of Jesus Christ that they imprisoned them, but the impact of the message was so powerful that 5000 people believed the message. Secondly, Peter and John, after imprisonment, came out even stronger and continued in the work of the Lord.

> Acts 4:2 (NIV) "2 They were greatly disturbed because
> the apostles were teaching the people, proclaiming
> in Jesus the resurrection of the dead."

> Acts 4:4 (NIV) "4 But many who heard the message
> believed; so the number of men who believed grew
> to about five thousand."

The undeniable impact was clear to everyone in Jerusalem and beyond. More and more people believed in the Lord, both as a result of them seeing the demonstration of the Power of God, as well as hearing the Message that was delivered by the Apostles.

> Acts 5:12 (NIV) The Apostles Heal Many "12 The
> apostles performed many signs and wonders
> among the people. And all the believers used to
> meet together in Solomon's Colonnade."

> Acts 5:14-15 (NIV) 14 Nevertheless, more and more men
> and women believed in the Lord and were added to

their number. 15 As a result, people brought the sick into the streets and laid them on beds and mats so that at least Peter's shadow might fall on some of them as he passed by.

### The early Believers also preached everywhere

The early Believers spread the Word of God everywhere they went. The Gospel was preached everywhere. Preaching is bringing the message that Jesus is the Son of God, and by faith in Him as your Lord and Saviour, He can save you.

> Acts 8:4 (NIV) "4 Those who had been scattered preached the word wherever they went."

> Acts 11:19-21 (NIV) "19 Now those who had been scattered by the persecution that broke out when Stephen was killed traveled as far as Phoenicia, Cyprus and Antioch, spreading the word only among Jews. 20 Some of them, however, men from Cyprus and Cyrene, went to Antioch and began to speak to Greeks also, telling them the good news about the Lord Jesus. 21 The Lord's hand was with them, and a great number of people believed and turned to the Lord."

We see how the Words of Jesus came into fulfillment through these Believers, as they became witnesses in Judea, Samaria and into the ends of the earth. Here we have an account of them preaching to Greeks and later on to Samaritans as well.

### Philip preached to the Samaritans

Philip was one of the Believers who got scattered through the persecution that broke out in Jerusalem. Instead of shrinking back, they went and spread the Gospel everywhere, even to the Samaritans, which was totally cross-cultural for them at that time.

> Acts 8:5 (NIV) "5 Philip went down to a city in Samaria and proclaimed the Messiah there."

> Acts 8:12 (NIV) "12 But when they believed Philip as he proclaimed the good news of the kingdom of God and the name of Jesus Christ, they were baptized, both men and women."

> Acts 8:25 (NIV) "25 After they had further proclaimed the word of the Lord and testified about Jesus, Peter and John returned to Jerusalem, preaching the gospel in many Samaritan villages."

**Paul immediately started preaching when he got** _____

The Apostle Paul, when He came to the Lord, immediately started preaching and proving that Jesus was the Messiah.

> Acts 9:20 (NIV) "20 At once he began to preach in the synagogues that Jesus is the Son of God."

***It is this obedient acting on the "Great Commission" that changed the entire world for Jesus.*** In Acts Chapter 16 we see another example of the impact of *"preaching"* the Gospel and Witnessing for the Lord Jesus. After Paul had his *"Macedonian Vision"* him and his companions set out for Macedonia to preach the Good News of Jesus.

> Acts 16:10 (NIV) "10 After Paul had seen the vision, we got ready at once to leave for Macedonia, concluding that God had called us to preach the gospel to them."

Acts 16:13-14 (NIV) "13 On the Sabbath we went outside
the city gate to the river, where we expected to find
a place of prayer. We sat down and began to speak
to the women who had gathered there. 14 One of
those listening was a woman from the city of
Thyatira named Lydia, a dealer in purple cloth.
She was a worshiper of God. The Lord opened her
heart to respond to Paul's message."

What we learn from the *"Witnessing"* through the lives of the
Apostles and the Believers in Acts are that they *"preached"* every-
where and that, *"the Lord"* truly *"worked with them to confirm the
Word"*.

**How can we put this Spiritual Discipline into practice?**

1. Make the "_____" your life's mission.

This means that you commit to embrace all the different aspects
of the Great Commission and fulfill it daily. It is the most natural
thing for new Believers to share their newfound faith in Jesus. I
encourage you to make this a lifelong mission and discipline of yours
to share your faith with others.

2. Make a commitment to put on the "_____ of preparedness"
to share your faith.

We are encouraged to put on the *"Full Armour of God"* daily. One
of the essential parts of the *"Armour of God"* is the *"Shoes of preparedness"*. Being prepared brings within us an expectation to keep our
eyes open for when the opportunity arises.

Being prepared also makes us less anxious when we have an
opportunity to share. Being prepared also makes us also bolder and
more confident since we expect to see how the Lord will open their
hearts to receive Him as their Lord and Savior.

> Ephesians 6:15 (NIV) "15 and with your feet fitted with
> the readiness that comes from the gospel of peace."

> Ephesians 6:15 (BBE) "15 Be ready with the good news
> of peace as shoes on your feet;"

Our preparation for each day should include a readiness to share the Hope we have in Jesus, whilst attending to keep our good behavior.

> 1 Peter 3:15-16 (NIV) "15 But in your hearts set apart
> Christ as Lord. Always be prepared to give an
> answer to everyone who asks you to give the reason
> for the hope that you have. But do this with
> gentleness and respect, 16 keeping a clear
> conscience, so that those who speak maliciously
> against your good behavior in Christ may be
> ashamed of their slander."

### 3. Learn how to share the Gospel like the Apostles did?

One of the top reasons why people do not share their faith, according to research by Lesli White from Beliefnet.com[1], is that people *"don't feel that they are knowledgeable"* to share the Gospel.

### The Gospel

The strategy and content that the Apostles and first Believers used to share the Gospel is well noted and contained in the New Testament. It was Biblically founded and intentionally pursued under the Power of the Holy Spirit. They used the Word of God in almost every account of witnessing about Jesus, and strongly depended on the Holy Spirit to bring conviction, and on the Lord to confirm His Word through Signs and Wonders. They pleaded with the listeners to be reconciled with God, to repent of their sins, and to accept Jesus Christ as Lord.

The Apostle Paul, in his address to the Church in Corinth, reminds them of the Gospel message by which they were saved:

> 1 Corinthians 15:1-8 (NIV) 1 Now, brothers, I want to remind you of the gospel I preached to you, which you received and on which you have taken your stand. 2 By this gospel you are saved, if you hold firmly to the word, I preached to you. Otherwise, you have believed in vain. 3 For what I received I passed on to you as of first importance : that Christ died for our sins according to the Scriptures,4 that he was buried, that he was raised on the third day according to the Scriptures, 5 and that he appeared to Peter, and then to the Twelve. 6 After that, he appeared to more than five hundred of the brothers at the same time, most of whom are still living, though some have fallen asleep. 7 Then he appeared to James, then to all the apostles, 8 and last of all he appeared to me also, as to one abnormally born."

*The Gospel is about Jesus Christ, who died for our sins, in our place, to save us, but then rose from the dead and is alive.* We now serve the living God! The validation of the Scriptures is remarkable throughout this message and throughout the preaching of Jesus, His Disciples and the numerous accounts of where we read of the Believers preaching.

**Christ died for our sins, according to the Scriptures.**

Christ died for our sins when we were still dead in our sins. We all sinned and need a Savior. Christ is our Savior.

Isaiah 53:5 (NIV) "5 But he was pierced for our
transgressions, he was crushed for our iniquities;
the punishment that brought us peace was upon
him, and by his wounds we are healed."

John 1:29 (NIV) "29 The next day John saw Jesus
coming toward him and said, "Look, the Lamb of
God, who takes away the sin of the world!"

1 Peter 2:24 (NIV) "24 He himself bore our sins in his
body on the tree, so that we might die to sins and
live for righteousness; by his wounds you have
been healed."

**Christ rose from the dead to offer us a living hope and eternal life.**

We believe that Christ was buried, and then rose from the dead.
He is alive and offers eternal life to all who believe in Him. We live
this life for Him so that we will live with Him for eternity.

1 Corinthians 15:19-20, 22 (NIV) 19 If only for this life we
have hope in Christ, we are to be pitied more than
all men. 20 But Christ has indeed been raised from
the dead, the firstfruits of those who have fallen
asleep. 22 For as in Adam all die, so in Christ all
will be made alive."

John 3:16 (NIV) "16 "For God so loved the world that he
gave his one and only Son, that whoever believes in
him shall not perish but have eternal life."

John 6:40 (NIV) "40 For my Father's will is that
everyone who looks to the Son and believes in him
shall have eternal life, and I will raise him up at the
last day."

**Christ is coming back again to take us to be with Him forever.**

Jesus is coming back! He is coming back to bring us to be with Him forever. He is also coming to reward us for our walk in Him. We will all stand before Him, some to receive their eternal reward and some to be sent into eternal damnation.

> Matthew 16:27 (NIV) "27 For the Son of Man is going to come in his Father's glory with his angels, and then he will reward each person according to what he has done."

> John 14:3 (NIV) "3 And if I go and prepare a place for you, I will come back and take you to be with me that you also may be where I am."

> 1 Thessalonians 4:16-17 (NIV) "16 For the Lord himself will come down from heaven, with a loud command, with the voice of the archangel and with the trumpet call of God, and the dead in Christ will rise first. 17 After that, we who are still alive and are left will be caught up together with them in the clouds to meet the Lord in the air. And so we will be with the Lord forever."

**We receive Him as Lord by confessing our sins and ask Him to be our Lord.**

We receive forgiveness when we repent and confess our sins. His blood washes and cleanses us.

> Romans 10:9 (NIV) "9 That if you confess with your mouth, "Jesus is Lord," and believe in your heart that God raised him from the dead, you will be saved."

Peter concluded his message on the Day of Pentecost with a Call to Repentance.

> Acts 2:38 (NIV) "38 Peter replied, "Repent and be baptized, every one of you, in the name of Jesus Christ for the forgiveness of your sins. And you will receive the gift of the Holy Spirit.""

Jesus Himself taught this Gospel message to His Disciples.

> Luke 24:46-47 (NIV) 46 He told them, "This is what is written: The Christ will suffer and rise from the dead on the third day, 47 and repentance and forgiveness of sins will be preached in his name to all nations, beginning at Jerusalem.

**The Gospel Message should be encased by the _____ of God**

Whenever Jesus preached, He referenced the Word of God. When Peter stood up on the Day of Pentecost and delivered that first Gospel Message, it was encased in Scriptural references. Twice in the first message he referenced the Scriptures.

> Acts 2:14, 16 (NIV) "14 Then Peter stood up with the Eleven, raised his voice and addressed the crowd: "Fellow Jews and all of you who live in Jerusalem, let me explain this to you; listen carefully to what I say. 16 No, this is what was spoken by the prophet Joel:"

> Acts 2:25 (NIV) "25 David said about him: ""I saw the Lord always before me. Because he is at my right hand, I will not be shaken.""

When Peter and John spoke in the Colonnade of Solomon when

Peter healed the cripple man, he encased it in references to Moses and the Prophets.

> Acts 3:22-23 (NIV) "22 For Moses said, 'The Lord your God will raise up for you a prophet like me from among your own people; you must listen to everything he tells you. 23 Anyone who does not listen to him will be completely cut off from among his people.'"

> Acts 3:24-25 (NIV) "24 "Indeed, all the prophets from Samuel on, as many as have spoken, have foretold these days. 25 And you are heirs of the prophets and of the covenant God made with your fathers. He said to Abraham, 'Through your offspring all peoples on earth will be blessed.'"

When Peter and John were brought before the Sanhedrin because of their preaching and the healing miracle of the cripple man, Peter referenced the Scriptures.

> Acts 4:10-12 (NIV 1984) "10 then know this, you and all the people of Israel: It is by the name of Jesus Christ of Nazareth, whom you crucified but whom God raised from the dead, that this man stands before you healed. 11 He is "'the stone you builders rejected, which has become the capstone.'12 Salvation is found in no one else, for there is no other name under heaven given to men by which we must be saved.'"

When Stephen spoke in Acts 7, he referenced the Word of God throughout his message. When Philip spoke to the Eunuch when the Holy Spirit directed him to go there, the Message was encased in Scripture.

The word of God is truly "*Living*" and "*Active*" and able to work Powerfully in us. The more we allow it on our lips we unlock its Power to bring change and transformation in the lives of people around us.

**The Gospel should be centered on Jesus Christ as the ____ of God.**

Whenever the Apostles and first Believers preached and shared the Gospel it was always centered on Jesus Christ. The whole Gospel centers on the Salvatory Work of Jesus Christ on the cross of Calvary. It's not about you or me; it's about Jesus, and us putting our faith in Him.

> Acts 2:22-24 (NIV 1984) "22 "Men of Israel, listen to this: Jesus of Nazareth was a man accredited by God to you by miracles, wonders and signs, which God did among you through him, as you yourselves know.23 This man was handed over to you by God's set purpose and foreknowledge; and you, with the help of wicked men, put him to death by nailing him to the cross. 24 But God raised him from the dead, freeing him from the agony of death, because it was impossible for death to keep its hold on him."

> Acts 2:32-33 (NIV 1984) "32 God has raised this Jesus to life, and we are all witnesses of the fact. 33 Exalted to the right hand of God, he has received from the Father the promised Holy Spirit and has poured out what you now see and hear."

At every juncture Peter, and the other Believers witnessed about Jesus, the Resurrected Christ.

Acts 3:16 (NIV 1984) "16 By faith in the name of Jesus, this man whom you see and know was made strong. It is Jesus' name and the faith that comes through him that has given this complete healing to him, as you can all see."

Acts 3:18-20 (NIV 1984) "18 But this is how God fulfilled what he had foretold through all the prophets, saying that his Christ would suffer. 19 Repent, then, and turn to God, so that your sins may be wiped out, that times of refreshing may come from the Lord, 20 and that he may send the Christ, who has been appointed for you–even Jesus."

**The Gospel message is received by _____ in Jesus as Lord**

The Gospel is received by confession and by faith receiving Christ as Lord.

Romans 10:9-10 (NIV 1984) 9 That if you confess with your mouth, "Jesus is Lord," and believe in your heart that God raised him from the dead, you will be saved. 10 For it is with your heart that you believe and are justified, and it is with your mouth that you confess and are saved."

Romans 10:13 (NIV 1984) "13 for, "Everyone who calls on the name of the Lord will be saved.""

**The preaching of the Gospel was always accompanied by a strong sense of _____ on the hearers.**

When Peter stood up in the midst of the Twelve and preached on the Day of Pentecost, a deep conviction came on all those who heard the Word of God. It was this same strong conviction that accompanied their messages in the Synagogue and wherever they preached the Word. The Word of God is Living and active. The Gospel is the Power of God to change lives.

> Acts 2:37-40 (NIV 1984) 37 When the people heard this, they were cut to the heart and said to Peter and the other apostles, "Brothers, what shall we do?" 38 Peter replied, "Repent and be baptized, every one of you, in the name of Jesus Christ for the forgiveness of your sins. And you will receive the gift of the Holy Spirit. 39 The promise is for you and your children and for all who are far off–for all whom the Lord our God will call." 40 With many other words he warned them; and he pleaded with them, "Save yourselves from this corrupt generation.""

> Acts 11:21 (NIV 1984) "21 The Lord's hand was with them, and a great number of people believed and turned to the Lord."

When Paul wrote to the Church in Thessalonica, he reminded them of how they received the Gospel. They received it; *"with deep conviction"*.

> 1 Thessalonians 1:4-5 (NIV 1984) 4 For we know, brothers loved by God, that he has chosen you, 5 because our gospel came to you not simply with words, but also with power, with the Holy Spirit and with deep conviction. You know how we lived among you for your sake."

∾

## The Practical Gospel Message

Here is an easy to remember way of sharing the Gospel:

### 1. Opener

**Do you know Jesus Christ?**

**Can I tell you about Him?**

Remember, the Gospel is all about people putting their faith in Jesus Christ. It's not about them. Or about you, it's about Jesus. You desire to reconcile them to God through faith in Jesus. The moment we start witnessing about Him the Power of God to save people is activated and God starts working with you to open their hearts to save them. God needs a Messenger and the moment you become His Messenger, the Holy Spirit and Jesus start doing their part to bring conviction to save the hearers.

### 2. Man

Mankind is like sheep without a Shepherd. Mankind find themselves caught in their sins. Many pursue things that make them have a sense of feeling alive, but truly trying to deal with the sense of being empty and looking to find the purpose for existence. Many feel dead on the inside even though they might seem successful to others. The reason for this is found in the Bible.

All of us sinned and are dead in our sins. Adam and Eve sinned in Eden. Through their sin, sin and spiritual death came to all mankind. We are all Sinners and are in need of a Savior who can save us from our sin and give us life.

Romans 3:23 (NIV) "[23] for all have sinned and fall short of the glory of God"

1 Corinthians 15:22 (NIV) "22 For as in Adam all die, so
in Christ all will be made alive."

## 3. God

God loves us so much that he sent His Son to pay the price to redeem us of our sins. He now offers Salvation to all who accept and believe in His Son.

John 3:16 (NIV) "16 "For God so loved the world that he
gave his one and only Son, that whoever believes in
him shall not perish but have eternal life."

## 4. Jesus Christ

Jesus Christ is the Son of God, who was conceived by the Holy Spirit, and born of the Virgin Mary. He was crucified, and died for our sins, and was buried. On the third day He rose again, as victor over death, to give eternal life to all who would believe in Him.

Isaiah 53:5 (NIV) "5 But he was pierced for our
transgressions, he was crushed for our iniquities;
the punishment that brought us peace was upon
him, and by his wounds we are healed."

John 1:29 (NIV) "29 The next day John saw Jesus
coming toward him and said, "Look, the Lamb of
God, who takes away the sin of the world!"

We appropriate this gracious work of Christ by putting our Faith in Jesus Christ to save us.

## 5. *I Believe*

It is valuable that we declare our faith and what we believe. We are sharing our faith by declaring what we believe. We are witnessing when we declare our faith. Here is a version of the Apostles' Creed to which we subscribe. Learn this of by heart and simply state your faith.

> *I believe in God, the Father Almighty, Creator of heaven and earth.*
> *I believe in Jesus Christ, God's only Son, our Lord,*
> *who was conceived by the Holy Spirit, born of the Virgin Mary,*
> *suffered under Pontius Pilate, was crucified, died, and was buried;*
> *He descended to the dead. On the third day He rose again; He ascended into heaven,*
> *He is seated at the right hand of God, our Father, and He will come to judge the living and the dead.*
> *I believe in the Holy Spirit, And I believe in one holy Christian and apostolic Church, the communion of saints, the forgiveness of sins, the resurrection of the body, and life everlasting. Amen.*[2]

You might ask:

### *What must I do to believe in Jesus?*

## *Put your trust and faith in Jesus*

We are saved when we confess our sins, and confess our faith in Jesus Christ as Lord and Savior. Father God offered eternal life to all who would believe in His Son, Jesus Christ. When we repent of our sins, He forgives us and restores into a right relationship with God.

> Romans 10:9-10 (NIV 1984) 9 That if you confess with
> your mouth, "Jesus is Lord," and believe in your
> heart that God raised him from the dead, you will
> be saved. 10 For it is with your heart that you

believe and are justified, and it is with your mouth that you confess and are saved."

Romans 10:13 (NIV 1984) "13 for, "Everyone who calls on the name of the Lord will be saved.""

Acts 2:38 (NIV 1984) "38 Peter replied, "Repent and be baptized, every one of you, in the name of Jesus Christ for the forgiveness of your sins. And you will receive the gift of the Holy Spirit."

Once you shared with people on how to receive Jesus as their Lord and Savior, you can ask if they want to accept Jesus, and then you can ask them if you could lead them in a prayer for Salvation.

**Do you want to open your heart and ask Jesus into your life? May I lead you in a Prayer for Salvation?**

### Prayer of Salvation

*Father God in Heaven, I confess that I am a Sinner. I repent of my sins and ask for Your Forgiveness. I ask You to be my Lord and Savior. Please forgive me, save me from my sin, and make me Your Child today. Wash me with Your Blood, Cleanse me by the Power of Your Holy Spirit. In Jesus Name. Amen*

# PART II

## VALUES OF THE KINGDOM OF GOD

## 2

# WATCHFULNESS

**Definition:**

Watchfulness is the action and activity of paying close attention to one's own, and other's lives, especially as it impacts others positively for Christ's sake.

**Scripture:**

> Matthew 16:6 (NIV)
> "⁶ "Be careful," Jesus said to them. "Be on your guard against the yeast of the Pharisees and Sadducees."
> Matthew 16:11-12

> Mark 13:33, 35-36 (NIV)
> "³³ Be on guard! Be alert! You do not know when that time will come. ³⁵ "Therefore keep watch because you do not know when the owner of the house will come back—whether in the evening, or at

midnight, or when the rooster crows, or at
dawn. [36] If he comes suddenly, do not let him find
you sleeping.[37] What I say to you, I say to everyone:
'Watch!'"

Luke 12:15 (NIV), Titus 2:12, Hebrews 2:1-4 (NIV), Mark
14:38 (NIV), Acts 20:28 (NIV), 2 Corinthians
10:5 (NIV)

**Characteristic explained:**

Watchfulness is the act of being alert and observant: alert as to possible dangers and endangering situations or influences, and at the same time observant over one's own example in every life situation. Watchfulness is also defined and described by having a sense of alertness, paying attention, having a careful awareness, a mindfulness and readiness to apply oneself with keenness and vigilance. Watchfulness requires us to make a commitment to take unruly and wayward thoughts captive. Watchfulness is also the activity of applying caution and to be on your guard.

**Life Application:**

A question to ask is:

1. *How alert and observant am I to observe endangering influences?*
2. *How vigilant am I to set up a guard and protection over my life, and that of others, when I see endangering situations arise?*

One of the ways to harness oneself with Watchfulness is to daily put on the Armour of God. The mental and prayerful application of the Armour of God, over time, guards us, and prepares us to be more alert and aware to be watchful. For us as Believers it is also the daily awareness to expectantly wait for the return of our Lord. We should be ready when the Lord Jesus returns, He should find us busy with His work and applying ourselves to the tasks He gave us to do. Let us be watchful over our lives, as to be on guard to keep our lives pure and in right standing with God. Be watchful!

# 3

# PERSEVERANCE

**Definition:**

Perseverance is the inbred ability to endure through difficult and hard times. It is the continuing in the faith regardless of what challenges might be encountered.

**Scriptures:**

> Galatians 6:9 "And let us not be weary in well doing: for in due season we shall reap, if we faint not."
>
> Hebrews 12:1 (NIV) "¹² Therefore, since we are surrounded by such a great cloud of witnesses, let us throw off everything that hinders and the sin that so easily entangles. And let us run with perseverance the race marked out for us,"
>
> Romans 8:25 (NIV), James 1:2-4, 12 (NIV), 1 Timothy 4:15-16 (NIV), Hebrews 10:16-36

## Characteristic explained:

Perseverance is the determined heart attitude to endure, presses on, and persist in whatever difficult situation one might find yourself in. Perseverance requires drive, insistent determination, grit, persistence and sometimes-even stubbornness to not give up or to let go of what you stand for or believe in. Perseverance is closely connected to our ability to endure through challenging and testing situations. Perseverance is also connected to our ability to take our stand for what we believe in regardless of the attacks that might be launched against us. One of the outstanding values that Believers in Christ exhibit is their ability to stay the course regardless of the sometimes challenging and unfavourable circumstances they encounter or face.

## Life Application:

The question we need to ask ourselves is:

1. *How strong am I standing in my faith?*
2. *What am I prepared to do to not give up?*

Perseverance is making a pre-determined decision that you will do whatever it takes to defend your faith. Perseverance is taking a strong and firm stand for your values. Perseverance is applying faith and hope to everyday challenges. Believers persevere so that they might receive their promised reward. Think of a challenging situation you are in or are facing at the moment where you think it is impossible to have a suitable outcome or breakthrough, well, since your faith is tested, decide to not give up hope that what God promised in His Word, will come to pass.

## 4

---

## HONOURING

**Definition:**

*To show honour is to be respectful in gesture, words and behaviour.* Being respectful is to show honour, reverence and deference to those you honour.

**Scriptures:**

> John 5:23 (NIV) "23 that all may honor the Son just as
> they honor the Father. Whoever does not honor
> the Son does not honor the Father, who sent him."

> Matthew 15:4 (NIV) "⁴ For God said, 'Honor your father
> and mother' and 'Anyone who curses their father
> or mother is to be put to death.'
> Romans 13:7 (NIV), Romans 13:1-7, 1 Timothy 6:1 (NIV), 1
> Peter 2:17 (NIV), Leviticus 19:32 (NIV),
> 1 Thessalonians 5:12-13 (NIV), Ephesians 6:1-3 (NIV),
> Proverbs 3:9 (NIV), Isaiah 29:13 (NIV)

## Characteristic explained:

*We honour when we show respect*. Respect could be shown to God, His Words, His Servants, Elderly people, our Parents, people in official Governmental Positions, Teachers and also those earthly things entrusted to us. We honour when we submit, respect and show admiration to people or even things. Embracing this Kingdom value means that we show respect for God when we look after everything we have, since we see them as gifts and privileges from God. We honour when we give credit, pay tribute and show admiration. We honour when we act on principle, present ourselves with nobility and take pride in where we live and how we conduct ourselves with others. The fact is that all of us love to have people in our lives that take pride in what we do or what we accomplished. In this way we feel honored. We honour when we treat people as if it is a privilege for us to be associated with them, and have the pleasure of their company.

## Life Application:

We honour God when we credit Him for all He does in our lives. *Honour God!* Honour God, not just with your lips, but also from your heart. One of the ways in which we honour God is by returning to Him a tenth of all our income. Honour God by Tithing! We value honouring God when we uphold the Leaders of the Country we live in, up in our prayers and submit to their authority. Honour God by honouring the Leader in Government! Honour Governmental Leaders! Honour those who are over you in the Lord. Show them the highest respect, because of the Lord. Honour your Spiritual Leaders! Honour one another by being respectful. Be Respectful! Honour always brings you into the presence of those in high authority and Leadership. Keep along the pathways of honour and it will put you in good standing with those who high places. Never become too familiar!

# SUBMISSIVE

**Definition:**

*Submission is the self-determined subjection to the will of another.* For us as Believers it is primarily to submit ourselves, through thought, words and actions, to the Will and Word of God.

**Scriptures:**

> Hebrews 5:7-9 (NIV) "⁷ During the days of Jesus' life on
> earth, he offered up prayers and petitions with
> fervent cries and tears to the one who could save
> him from death, and he was heard because of his
> reverent submission. ⁸ Son though he was, he
> learned obedience from what he suffered ⁹ and,
> once made perfect, he became the source of eternal
> salvation for all who obey him."

> Hebrews 13:17 (NIV) "Obey them that have the rule
> over you, and submit yourselves: for they watch for

your souls, as they that must give account, that they may do it with joy, and not with grief: for that is unprofitable for you."

Romans 13:1 (NIV), Romans 13:5 (NIV), James 4:7 (NIV), James 4:9 (NIV), Proverbs 3:5-6 (NIV), 1 Peter 5:5-6 (NIV)

**Characteristic explained:**

For us as Believers, Submission is to subject oneself to the God, His Son, His Word, His Will, His Holy Spirit, His Leaders and His Guidance. To submit requires humility, obedience, compliance and willing following. Submission and Obedience could almost be used interchangeably within the context of the Kingdom of God Value System. It requires obedience to submit, and submission to obey everything the Lord taught us. There also exist a close relationship with the Value of Humility in Submission and Obedience. Submission requires us to consider the Will of God over that of ours. Submission requires adherence to the Bible, the Holy Spirit as well as those whom God placed over us in the Church.

**Life Application:**

The question is:

*How submitted am I to the Will of God?*

One way of developing this Value of Submission in our lives is of course to pray and meditate on it, especially when we pray the *"Our Father"* prayer. Jesus taught us in the *"Our Father"* prayer to pray: *"May Your Will be done, on earth as it is in Heaven"*. Submission starts with submitting to the Will and Purpose of God in our lives. No submission is truly possible if it is not rooted in our humble submission to God, however, if we truly submit ourselves to God, then all other requirements for submission will not be seen as unrealistic and legalistic Christian laws, but something we want to honour because of our love for the Lord. Pray for the Government of your nation. Pray for the Leaders God placed over you, at work, at school, and at your Church, and as you pray for them, also pledge your allegiance to their authority over you.

# PART III

## ASSIMILATION SHEET

### Spiritual Discipline: Witnessing

1. Did Jesus teach His Disciples on Servanthood? _____ If Yes, What did Jesus teach His Disciples on Witnessing? Provide Scripture.

_____

_____

_____

_____

2. Fill in the blank spaces! *Witnessing requires a commitment to both be a "* _____*" and "* _____*."*

3. Complete the sentence! Witnessing requires a commitment to both "preach" and "_____."

4. The Gospel is captured by Paul in what Scripture? Outline the Three Main Points of this Scripture? _____

_____

_____

_____

## Values of the Kingdom of God

4. Why is *"Watchfulness"* so valued as a Kingdom Value?

_____

_____

_____

_____

5. How can you *"Persevere"* more?

_____

_____

_____

_____

6. What does it mean to be *"Honouring"*?

_____

_____

_____

_____

7. What does it mean to be "Submissive"?

_____

_____

_____

_____

8. How can you model more *"Submissiveness"*?

_____

_____

_____

_____

# AFTERWORD

**Obedience**

In conclusion of Phase Two of Discipleship Journeys, let us consider a few essentials again.

## Jesus commissioned us to obey!

Firstly, Jesus taught His Disciples the *Spiritual Discipline of Obedience*. Part of the process of Discipleship is to teach our disciples *"to obey everything"* Jesus taught us.

> Matthew 28:20 (NKJV) "20 teaching them to observe all
> things that I have commanded you; and lo, I am
> with you always, even to the end of the age."
> Amen."

∾

Matthew 28:20 (The Passion Translation) " [20] And teach them to faithfully follow[i] all that I have commanded you. And never forget that I am with you every day, even to the completion of this age."

**Jesus modelled obedience.**

Jesus practiced and modelled obedience unto death. Our disciplines are not just for a season or for a specific event, but it is an inward aptitude of discipline for this life.

Philippians 2:8 (NKJV) "8 And being found in appearance as a man, He humbled Himself and became obedient to the point of death, even the death of the cross."

**Jesus was obedient unto death. He calls us to follow in His footsteps.**

John 14:23-24 (NIV) "23 Jesus replied, "Anyone who loves me will obey my teaching. My Father will love them, and we will come to them and make our home with them. 24 Anyone who does not love me will not obey my teaching. These words you hear are not my own; they belong to the Father who sent me."

*Jesus learnt obedience through His suffering.* Disciplining ourselves daily towards submission and obedience to the Word, Will and Purpose of God will most certainly unlock great favour and blessing over our lives. This is the Promise God gave us in Deuteronomy 28 verses 1-13, for full submission and obedience.

**Joshua and Caleb obeyed and conquered.**

*Joshua and Caleb had the faith to obey*, and therefor entered into the Promised land God promised them.

> Hebrews 4:2 (NIV) "[2] For we also have had the good news proclaimed to us, just as they did; but the message they heard was of no value to them, because they did not share the faith of those who obeyed."

When we combine our Faith in God with Obedience, we too will enter our Promised lands.

**Faith to Obey**

It takes faith to obey, and faith is expressed by the way we obey.

## Spiritual Maturity

*Putting things into practice and obeying God will bring us to spiritual Maturity.* No spiritual maturity is ever possible without practicing and living the values, and practicing the disciplines taught in this Discipleship Journey through the Teachings of Jesus and the Bible.

> Hebrews 5: 14 (NIV) "[14] But solid food is for the mature, who by constant use have trained themselves to distinguish good from evil."

> Hebrews 5:12-14 (AMPC) "[12] For even though by this time you ought to be teaching others, you actually need someone to teach you over again the very first principles of God's Word. You have come to need milk, not solid food. [13] For everyone who continues to feed on milk is obviously inexperienced and

unskilled in the doctrine of righteousness (of
conformity to the divine will in purpose, thought,
and action), for he is a mere infant [not able to talk
yet]! [14] But solid food is for full-grown men, for
those whose senses and mental faculties are
trained by practice to discriminate and distinguish
between what is morally good and noble and what
is evil and contrary either to divine or human law."

When we look at this portion in God's Word, we see a number of
essential truths that will bring us to Spiritual Maturity.

## 1. We need someone to teach us.

Hebrews 5:12 (AMPC) "[12] For even though by this time
you ought to be teaching others, you actually need
someone to teach you over again the very first
principles of God's Word. You have come to need
milk, not solid food."

The first is that *we all need*, as you did by going through this
course, *someone to teach you the elementary truths* of God's Word. In
this portion the writer to the Hebrews actually speaks in the negative
tone as he addresses Believers who were supposed to be Mature, and
Teachers of the truth, however, because *"they have become dull"* in
their *"[spiritual] hearing and sluggish [even slothful in achieving spiritual insight,"* they needed to be taught again. May we learn and keep
the things we have learned, *in practice*, in our lives.

## 2. Spiritual Maturity comes through conforming to the Will of God.

Hebrews 5:13 (AMPC) "[13] For everyone who continues
to feed on milk is obviously inexperienced and

unskilled in the doctrine of righteousness (of conformity to the divine will in purpose, thought, and action), for he is a mere infant [not able to talk yet]!"

Secondly, we learn that to be mature requires us to be experienced and skilled in *"the doctrine of righteousness"* which means that we have *"conformed to the divine will of God in purpose, thought and action"*. I want to encourage you to make a heartfelt decision to conform to the Will of God.

**Conforming means to imitate, follow and obey.** May we obey, follow and imitate the example set to us by our Lord and Saviour Jesus Christ. I love the expansion of the Amplified Bible when it says: *"conformed to the divine will of God in purpose, thought and action"*. Maturity comes to those who build the Spiritual values and disciplines into their lives purposefully, both in thought and in their actions.

### 3. Spiritual maturity comes by practice and training to discriminate and to distinguish.

> Hebrews 5:14 (AMPC) "14 But solid food is for full-
>     grown men, for those whose senses and mental
>     faculties are trained by practice to
>     discriminate and distinguish between what is
>     morally good and noble and what is
>     evil and contrary either to divine or human law."

In the third place we see that Spiritual maturity comes by practicing and training our *"senses and mental faculties"*, *"to discriminate and to distinguish"* between what is *"morally good and noble"*. For us, this is our desire to please the Lord in everything. What the Bible teaches us here is that we need to apply our senses and mental faculties to pursue Spiritual Maturity. Allow the Holy Spirit to speak to you and to have His way in developing and working in you. By taking these teaching of the Lord Jesus, and the Bible, and apply them as a standard by which we distinguish and assess our intentions, actions and practices, we will become mature and full-grown men in Christ.

One of the things that made the Disciples distinct from the rest of the people was that people could see in their actions that they have been with Jesus.

> Acts 4:13 (NIV) "[13] When they saw the courage of Peter and John and realized that they were unschooled, ordinary men, they were astonished and they took note that these men had been with Jesus."

*"When people look at our courage, our values, our disciplines, they must recognise that we are Followers and Believers in Jesus."*
*Hendrik J. Vorster*

### Conclusion on Spiritual Disciplines and Values

There are many spiritual disciplines to explore and assimilate into our daily lives. The Spiritual Disciplines of Fasting and Prayer, Stewardship, Simplicity, Servanthood, studying and meditating on the Word of God, are some of the most valued disciplines to uphold, however, none is possible without a commitment to Obey the Lord from your heart. You can read more on these in my Books: *"Values of the Kingdom of God"*, and *"Spiritual Disciplines of the Kingdom of God."* Spiritual disciplines will keep the fire of God burning ablaze inside of you.

Spiritual Disciplines and Values make up our emotional intelligence, and it is said to consist of a set of four skills that we can learn and develop. It's not some mystical wonder or giftedness, and if you commit yourself to develop it, it works transformational!

∼

1. Develop self-awareness
    2. Develop self-control
    3. Build your awareness of others
    4. Build and maintain relationships

Most people inadvertently do not develop or build these values and disciplines into their social and character development. I pray that you will see the value of developing and building these disciplines and values into your life, and that you too will enjoy the fruit of a God-honoring and developed character.

Shalom!

# OTHER BOOKS BY DR. HENDRIK J VORSTER

*Step One - Salvation Disciple Manual*

**Discipleship Foundation Series**
**Step One - Salvation**

This Course explores the *"How to"* be Born Again and to establish a solid Foundation for your faith in Jesus Christ. It is based on Hebrews chapter 6 verses 1 & 2, and explores:

Repentance of dead works,
Faith in God,
Baptisms,
Laying on of hands,
Resurrection of the dead, and
Eternal Judgement

*Free Video Teaching material* is available at www.discipleshipcourses.com *Disciple Manuals can be purchased* through our website: www.churchplantinginstitute.com or at www.amazon.com

*Step Two - Values and Spiritual Disciplines Disciple Manual*

**Discipleship Foundations Series Step Two - Values and Spiritual Disciplines Disciple Manual**

*By Dr. Hendrik J Vorster*

This Course explores the *"How to" develop spiritual disciplines* as well as *52 Values* Jesus taught. It is based on the teachings of Jesus to His Disciples, and explores:

**Spiritual Disciplines**

The disciplines we explore are: Reading, meditating on the Word of God, Prayer, Stewardship, Fasting, Servanthood, Simplicity, Worship, and Witnessing.

**Values of the Kingdom of God**

Humility, Mournfulness, meekness, Spiritual Passion, Mercifulness, Purity, Peacemaker, Patient endurance, Example, Custodian, Reconciliatory, Resoluteness, Loving, Discreetness, Forgiving, Kingdom of God Investor, God-minded, Kingdom of God prioritiser, Introspective, Persistent, Considerate, Conservative, Fruit-bearing, Practitioner, Accountability, Faithful, Childlikeness, Unity, Servanthood, Loyalty, Gratefulness, Stewardship, Obedience, Carefulness, Compassion, Caring, Confidence, Steadfastness, Contentment, Teachable, Deference, Diligence, Trustworthiness, Gentleness, Discernment, Truthfulness, Generous, Kindness, Watchfulness, Perseverance, Honouring and Submissive.

**This, Disciple Manual and Video Teaching materials** are available, for purchase, from www.discipleshipcourses.com our website: www.churchplantinginstitute.com or at www.amazon.com

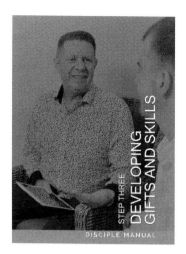

*Step Three - Developing Gifts and Skills*

**Discipleship Foundations Series Step Three - Developing Gifts and Skills**

This course is run through *five weekend encounters*. These weekend encounters have been designed to help Disciples discover their spiritual gifts, as well as learn skills to use their gifts, and to serve the Lord for the extension of His Kingdom. The Weekend Encounters are:

**Gifts Discovery Encounter**

We learn about Ministerial Office gifts, Service gifts, and Supernatural Spiritual Gifts. We discover our own gifts, and then learn How we may use them to build up the local Church.

**Survey of the Bible Weekend Encounter**

During this weekend we do a survey of the Bible, from Genesis to Revelation. We also learn about the History of the Bible as well as How we can make most of our time in the Word.

**Sharing your Faith Weekend Encounter**

During this weekend we learn about the Gospel message, and *How to share our faith* effectively.

**Overcoming Weekend Encounter**

During this weekend we deal with those **thistles and thorns** that smother the growth and harvest of the good seed sown into our lives. We address How to overcome fear, unforgiveness, lust and the cares of the world with faith and obedience.

**Shepherd Leader Weekend Encounter**

During this weekend encounter we learn about being a Good Shepherd, and How to best disciple in a small group.

**Teacher Manuals and Video Teachings** are available.

## Discipleship Foundations Series Step Four - Discipling Fruit-Producers

*Step Four - Fruitfulness*

*By Dr. Hendrik J Vorster*

We were saved to serve. This course has been designed to mobilise Believers, from Learners to Practitioners. These sessions have been prepared for individual use, with those who are bearing fruit, and want to produce more fruit. Developing these areas in a sustained and systematic manner will ensure both fruitfulness and multiplication. Attending to these areas will ensure that you bear lasting fruit.

We explore:

1. Introduction.
2. Walking with purpose.
3. Build purposeful relationships. Finding Worthy Men
4. Priesthood. Praying effectively for those entrusted to you.
5. Caring compassionately.
6. Walking worthily.
7. Walking in the Spirit.
8. Practicing hospitality.

**This, Teacher Manual and Video Teaching materials** are available, for purchase, from www.discipleshipcourses.com our website: www.churchplantinginstitute.com or at www.amazon.com

*Step Five - Multiplication - Dr. Hendrik J Vorster*

## Discipleship Foundations Series
## Step Five - Multiplication

*By Dr Hendrik J Vorster*

This course was designed to assist fruit-producing disciples to live a life that will encourage a lifetime of fruitfulness. It will also give our disciples skills and guidelines to navigate their disciples through seasons of challenge and growth. This course is packed with Leadership advancing principles. The more these areas are addressed and encouraged, the more we will experience growth and multiplication.

We explore:

1. Vision and dreams.
2. Set Godly Goals.
3. Character development
4. Gifts development - Impartation and Activation
5. Fruitfulness comes through constant challenge.
6. Relationships - Family, Children and Friends
7. The Power of encouragement
8. Finances - Personal and Ministry finances
9. Dealing with setbacks
- *How to deal with failure?*
- *How to deal with betrayal?*
- *How to deal with rejection?*
- *How to deal with trials?*
- *How to deal with despondency?*
10. Eternal rewards

**Teacher Manuals and Video Teachings** are available.

# Values
## of the
# Kingdom
## of
# God

Dr. Hendrik J. Vorster

**Values of the Kingdom of God**
*By Dr. Hendrik J Vorster*

Everyone desires to be known as a pleasant to be around with kind of person. This book helps you develop values towards such a godly character. This book explores 52 Values of the Kingdom of God.

**Books** are available from our website: www.churchplantinginstitute.com or at www.amazon.com

## SPIRITUAL DISCIPLINES
### OF THE
## KINGDOM
### OF
## GOD

Spiritual Disciplines of the Kingdom of God
*By Dr. Hendrik J Vorster*

Every Believer desires to be a Fruit-producing branch in the Vineyard of our Lord. Developing spiritual disciplines is to develop spiritual roots from which our faith can draw sap to grow strong and fruit-bearing branches. This Book explores Nine Spiritual Disciplines of the Kingdom of God.

**Books** are available from our website: www.churchplantinginstitute.com or at www.amazon.com

# Church Planting

How to plant a dynamic church

Dr. Hendrik J. Vorster

*Foreword by: Dr. Yonggi Cho*

*Church Planting - Dr Hendrik J Vorster*

**Church Planting - How to plant a dynamic, disciple-making church**

*By Dr Hendrik J Vorster*

This is a handbook for those who wish to plant a disciple-making church. This book explores every aspect of church planting, and is widely used in over 70 Nations on 6 Continents. Here is a list of the areas that are explored:

1. The challenge to plant New Churches
2. Phases of Church Planting
3. Phase One of Church Planting - The Calling, Vision and Preparation Phase
4. The Call to Church Planting
5. Twelve Characteristics of Church Planting Leaders
6. Church Planting Terminology
7. Phase Two of Church Planting - Discipleship
8. The Process of Discipleship
9. Phase Three of Church Planting - Congregating the Discipleship Groups
10. Understanding Church Planting Finances
11. Understanding Church staff
12. Phase Four of Church Planting - Ministry development and Church Launching Phase
13. Understanding and Implementing Systems
14. Phase Five of Church Planting - Multiplication
15. Understanding the challenges in Church Planting
16. How to succeed in Church Planting
17. How to plant a House Church

**This Book, and Video Teaching materials,** are available for purchase, from www.churchplantingcourses.com or through our website, www.churchplantinginstitute.com or at www.amazon.com

# NOTES

## I. Introduction

1. Wilson Todd, Dream Big, pg. 29, iBooks
2. Wilson Todd, Dream Big, pg. 29, iBooks
3. Ralph W. Neighbour Jr., Life Basic Training, back page, Touch Publications

## 1. Reading, meditating and practicing the Word of God.

1. Miller & Huber, Stephen & Robert (2003). *The Bible: the making and impact on the Bible a history*. England: Lion Hudson. p. 21. ISBN 0-7459-5176-7.
2. https://en.wikipedia.org/wiki/Nevi%27im
3. Neusner, Jacob, The Talmud Law, Theology, Narrative: A Sourcebook. University Press of America, 2005
4. Coogan, Michael D. *A Brief Introduction to the Old Testament: the Hebrew Bible in its Context*. Oxford University Press. 2009; p. 5
5. Coogan, Michael D. *A Brief Introduction to the Old Testament: the Hebrew Bible in its Context*. Oxford University Press. 2009; p. 5
6. [6] What the Bible is All About Visual Edition by Henrietta C. Mears – Gospel Light Publications, 2007. pp. 438–39
7. Bart D. Ehrman (1997). *The New Testament: A Historical Introduction to the Early Christian Writings*. Oxford University Press. p. 8. ISBN 978-0-19-508481-8.
8. *Saint Justin Martyr*, Encyclopædia Britannica, Inc.

## 1. Witnessing

1. https://www.beliefnet.com/faiths/christianity/galleries/7-reasons-christians-dont-share-their-faith.
2. https://en.wikipedia.org/wiki/Apostles%27_Creed